The Big
CHOCOLATE
Cookbook

The Big
CHOCOLATE
Cookbook

by Gertrude Parke

Galahad Books • New York City

This edition published in the United States of America in 1984 by
Galahad Books
95 Madison Avenue
New York, NY 10016
By arrangement with Gertrude Parke

Library of Congress Catalog Card Number: 81-70445
ISBN: 0-88365-609-4
Printed in the United States of America

CONTENTS

THEOBROMA CACAO
"FOOD OF THE GODS"

*T*HUS LINNAEUS, the Swedish botanist, named chocolate, that divine sustenance for us mortals, which has delighted people everywhere on earth and has become the favorite flavor of millions.

Picture, if you can bear it, life without chocolate. Imagine existence without those beguiling chocolate desserts, those lucious candies, sauces, and syrups, all of which add charm and flavor to our daily fare, and the lack of which would form an intolerable privation.

How could the most carefully contrived repast end with that ideal perfection one always hopes for, unless it is terminated by a delicately fragile chocolate soufflé, fashioned by a dexterous cook, and so expertly timed that it emerges from the oven at exactly the right moment, light as a cloud, to be complemented by chocolate sauce, laced with a dash or two of crème de cacao?

Imagine a picnic without a four-layered devil's food, lavishly iced with the darkest of creamy chocolate icings! The cake itself melts delectably on the tongue, and the frosting—ah!—such subtle blending of flavors, such a marvel of chocolate velvet, that one can't believe it and tries another mouthful to be sure.

How would our littlest tots survive without that sustaining chocolate drink after school, to soothe the ever-present pangs of hunger and to restore the energy depleted by a day of wrestling with the three R's; or that chocolate ice-cream cone, so eagerly licked on a hot summer's day?

What about chocolate sodas, éclairs, hot fudge sundaes, chocolate *pots-de-crème*, and so on and so on. Could we survive without these? Possibly—but enjoy life? . . . never!

Columbus is credited by some with bringing this culinary marvel, in the form of the small dark beans we now call cacao, along with other treasures, to lay at the feet of King Ferdinand and Queen Isabella of Spain. Others say that Cortés is entitled to this well-deserved praise. Be that as it may, we reap the benefit today, and each of us happily consumes about four pounds of cocoa products a year. Personally, I feel this figure must have been underestimated, unless some individuals are deprived of their quota due to my inordinate love of chocolate.

History tells us that in 1519 Cortés and his soldiers encountered chocolate for the first time at the court of Montezuma. They were present at a strange ritual when Montezuma, high on his throne, repeatedly raised a golden ceremonial goblet to his lips, while his subjects watched in silent reverence. What was this drink, served always in golden goblets? What significance did it hold in this strange barbaric land?

Later, the Spaniards, too, were served bowls of this exciting liquid. It was called *chocolatl*, they learned, meaning "warm liquid," and the tree bearing the seeds from which the drink was made was called *cacahuatl*, or "bitter juice."

The Aztecs believed that one of their prophets had brought the seeds from Paradise and had sown them in his garden, and that their consumption conveyed universal wisdom and knowledge. So the cacao bean assumed an importance in their religious life, and was considered of such value that it became a medium of exchange: a live slave, for example, could be purchased for one hundred beans; a turkey, for four. So they could either drink their cocoa beans or spend them.

The chocolate which the Aztecs drank, we are told, was unsweetened. Other uses for this product were developed, such as the *mole* sauce, created in the 19th century by a nun in Puebla, which is served on turkey or wild boar. Do not be misled into thinking of this as a chocolate sauce such as we are accustomed to. It is a blend of chilies, onions, sesame seeds, nuts, and unsweetened chocolate. The result is a rich sauce, spicy and tasty, having an intriguing flavor which is enjoyed by the most discriminating palate. I urge you to try it.

In Mexico today chocolate to drink is prepared in an unusual way. The roasted cocoa beans are ground with spices, sugar, and toasted nuts. This mixture is warmed and mixed with beaten eggs, making a pastelike mixture. This is shaped into balls or cakes, then cooled and stored. When a hot drink is called for, the cakes are melted in hot water, and the liquid is whipped to a froth. Another favorite Mexican drink, *champurrado*, is made by grinding maize flour, chocolate cakes, and sugar. Milk and vanilla are added, then the drink is warmed and beaten until it is foaming.

Little did Cortés think, when he extracted a tribute of three hundred pounds of cacao beans from Montezuma, that he was sending to Spain the start of a craze for chocolate which would spread all over the world, and bring pleasure to millions of people, old and young, who will ask for "anything, so long as it's chocolate."

In writing to his Emperor, Charles V, Cortés described

chocolatl as "the divine drink . . . which builds up resistance and fights fatigue."

The use of chocolate became accepted in Spain, where it was served as a sweetened frothy beverage, sometimes with the addition of cinnamon and vanilla. In fact, it became so popular that Spain planted cacao in its colonial possessions, thus creating a most profitable business which they kept to themselves for nearly a hundred years.

Gradually chocolate spread to Italy and France, where it became rather a scandalous sensation. It was condemned as "unwholesome," and called "the beverage of Satan" by churchmen, but was served enthusiastically at the French court, where it was considered an aphrodisiac. This seems unbelievable today, when cocoa is the prescribed drink for every innocent child of tender years, and is, as well, the comfort of the aging.

To quote Brillat-Savarin, ". . . it [chocolate] agrees with the feeblest stomachs, and has proved beneficial to chronic maladies." Thomas Jefferson later spoke of the ". . . superiority of chocolate both for health and nourishment."

A famous Florentine merchant of the 16th century, Francesco Carletti, traveled around the world and reported, ". . . once one is accustomed to it [chocolate], it is hard to give up drinking every morning . . . or in the evening . . . and particularly when one is traveling." An example to emulate.

By 1707, chocolate had become an accepted drink in England, where it was served in shops such as The Cocoa Tree, where men gathered for political discussion. Vanilla, cloves, cinnamon, or aniseed was sometimes added to give a fillip to the drink.

So far, no one had invented any form of chocolate other than the drink, thus to pave the way for those marvelous chocolate desserts and confections which leave a lingering deliciousness on our palates and in our memories.

It was not until 1876 that milk chocolate was created in Switzerland, using basically the process we use today. The roasted cocoa beans are milled, producing chocolate liquor from which all chocolate is made. The cocoa butter content of this liquor is about 55 per cent, and this proportion is maintained in baking chocolate. This liquor is poured into hot molds to harden, and these rich brown slabs we transform into luscious chocolate icing, or wonderful hot fudge sauce for spooning over ice cream, preferably chocolate ice cream!

To make cocoa, the chocolate liquor is pumped into presses and some of the cocoa butter is squeezed out. The resulting cake-like substance is then ground and sifted, and becomes cocoa. This makes possible that dark delicious devil's-food cake, and a hot frothy cup of cocoa to sip before the fire on a frosty winter's evening.

The Dutch developed a way of treating cocoa with alkali to produce a darker product with a different flavor, while Switzerland is noted for its chocolate of velvety smoothness.

Milk chocolate is made by adding whole milk solids, sugar, additional cocoa butter, and vanilla to chocolate liquor. Sweet and semisweet chocolate are made in the same way, but omitting the milk. So we have chocolate bits for cookies, chocolate curls to top a grasshopper pie, and chocolate candy bars for those times when we cannot bear to go a minute longer without indulging ourselves with a bit of that heavenly flavor.

Chocolate was unknown in the American colonies all the time it was becoming the rage in Europe, until fishermen from Gloucester, Massachusetts, accepted cacao beans as payment for cargo in tropical America, thus bringing the beans to our country for the first time. In 1765 the first chocolate factory was established in New England, and from then on we became a nation of chocolate enthusiasts.

The value of chocolate as a source of quick energy has long been recognized. For Queen Victoria's troops, Civil War soldiers, and in the 20th century through two world wars, the records show that chocolate was standard in the military diet. Today's D ration includes three 4-ounce chocolate bars.

Athletes have long been aware of the excellent properties of chocolate. Coaches frequently supply their players with chocolate, not only because it boosts energy, but also because it relieves the pangs of hunger some athletes suffer because they eat lightly before an important sports event.

Businessmen keep candy bars at hand to fight fatigue at the end of a long grueling day; their office and factory workers follow suit, finding that chocolate raises their blood-sugar level, and so helps them to stay alert during that afternoon slump.

The housewife can renew her flagging energy with a fragrant cup of cocoa in the middle of the morning. There is a variety of chocolate drinks to intrigue her. She could try Cocoa Mexican Style, or a Chocolate Orange Soda. Brandied Cocoa is a treat on a blustery winter's day, while a Chocolate Eggnog is rich and nourishing. With any of these, she could serve some delicious chocolate breads—Holiday Bread, Chocolate Tea Rolls, or Chocolate Almond Cake.

A box of chocolate confections at hand for nibbling is a joy at any time. A box of chocolate cookies in the freezer takes care of many an emergency.

Every hostess has a desire to serve an exceptional dessert to delight her guests. What a bewildering array there is! She can choose from the fabulous *Torten*, the chocolate cakes beyond compare, the dulcet *pots-de-crème*, the refrigerator desserts to be made ahead of time, or the variety of entrancing pies made with a chocolate crust or filling, or both, and possibly topped with chilled whipped cream and decorated with chocolate curls or cutouts to present a charming and mouth-watering picture.

A towering *croquembouche*, beautifully glazed, is worthy of the most formal of dinner parties; a *bombe*, magnificently layered with a chocolate mousse sparked with more than a generous touch of cognac, a raspberry sherbet, rosy and fragrant, and a delightful contrast to the pistachio parfait forming the center of the mold, makes a sensational ending to a memorable meal.

I know of no one who actually dislikes chocolate—most people are simply mad about it. Personally, I could live happily on a sequence of chocolate desserts, and can attest that if one is a chocolate enthusiast one does not ponder, "What sort of dessert can I make today?" but merely, "What can I make that's chocolate?"

And you reach for this book.

CHOCOLATE—ITS MANY USES

*T*HERE IS A VARIETY of chocolate and cocoa products to choose from and their uses are seemingly endless.

ALL ABOUT CHOCOLATE

Unsweetened chocolate, also referred to as bitter chocolate or baking chocolate, begins as pure chocolate liquid, called liquor by the manufacturer, which is heated and then poured in molds to cool and harden. It comes in pound and half-pound blocks, divided into either one-ounce or half-ounce squares for your convenience.

The liquid chocolate now available can be substituted, ounce for ounce in most recipes. It comes in one-ounce envelopes. This product is made from cocoa and cocoa butter or vegetable fats If it seems a little too stiff to press out of the envelope when you start to use it, just run hot water over it for a few seconds and the chocolate will come out readily.

Note: All recipes in this book use unsweetened chocolate unless otherwise specified.

Cocoa is the powder made from chocolate after most of the cocoa butter has been removed. It can be used in place of unsweetened chocolate in most recipes, by substituting 3 tablespoon of cocoa, plus one tablespoon of fat (vegetable shortening), for each ounce of chocolate. (Do not substitute semisweet chocolate or milk chocolate for baking chocolate.)

Cocoa comes in one-pound and half-pound containers, usually. It is used for baking, candy-making, and drinking.

Sweet chocolate is made from chocolate liquor with sugar and extra cocoa butter added. It comes in bars and can be used either for cooking or eating.

Germans Sweet Chocolate comes in 4-ounce packages and may be used for cooking or eating.

Semisweet chocolate is made from chocolate liquor with some sugar added. Chocolate bits, dainties, and morsels made from this come in 6-ounce and 12-ounce packages, which measure one cup and two cups, respectively.

Semisweet chocolate is also available in bars, marked into one-ounce squares as is the unsweetened chocolate.

Milk chocolate is made like semisweet, but has milk added. It is most generally used for eating and comes in a variety of forms.

Dutch process cocoa and chocolate has been treated to produce a darker and richer cocoa. This can be used in any recipe calling for regular cocoa or chocolate.

Storing chocolate. Keep chocolate on your pantry shelf where the temperature does not exceed 75° F. A higher temperature will change the color of the chocolate, due to the melting of the cocoa butter in the chocolate, although neither the flavor nor the quality is affected.

To melt chocolate. Remember that it scorches easily, so that it must be melted over low heat. Melt it in the top of a double boiler over hot but not boiling water. If you have a thermostatically controlled burner on a gas range, you can safely melt chocolate over direct heat, setting the burner at LOW or KEEP WARM. If, when melting semisweet chocolate, you find that it stiffens, correct this by adding 1 to 2 tablespoons of vegetable shortening to each 6 ounces of chocolate.

TIPS FOR BETTER BAKING

FLOUR. Use all-purpose flour. This should be sifted before spooning it lightly into a measuring cup, then level it off without shaking or packing it down.

If the recipe calls for cake flour, and you are using all-purpose flour, remove 2 tablespoons per cup used.

If the recipe calls for instantized flour, you may use all-purpose flour instead.

SUGAR. Confectioners' sugar, often referred to as XXXX sugar, should be sifted to insure smoothness. To measure this as well as granulated sugar, spoon it into a measuring cup and level it off. For smaller measures, use nested cups or measuring spoons.

For brown sugar, pack firmly into the measuring cup or spoon and then level it off. Granulated brown or brownulated sugar needs no packing.

SHORTENING is most easily measured by the water-replacement method. For instance, if ⅔ cup is called for, subtract this from 1 cup; run cold water in a measuring cup to the ⅓ mark, thus leaving room for the amount of shortening (⅔ cup) specified. Spoon the shortening in until the water reaches the 1-cup mark. Pour off water before using the shortening.

For smaller amounts of soft shortening, such as ¼ cup, it is easier to measure 4 level tablespoons. Butter measures are easier: 1 stick of butter = ¼ pound, or 8 tablespoons, or ½ cup.

VANILLA. Always use pure vanilla extract. Its extra cost is a minor matter compared to the improvement in flavor. In some places, drug stores carry fine vanilla.

Add vanilla only to cool ingredients since it has an alcohol base and heat releases not only fragrance, but flavor as well.

A vanilla bean is probably the best source of vanilla flavor. A piece of it may be heated with the liquid to be used in a dessert. Remove the bean, dry it, and use it again. (This, of course, cannot go on indefinitely. The bean will eventually lose its flavoring quality.) Or the bean may be split and the center scraped into a cold dessert and mixed in.

Try making vanilla sugar to flavor your puddings. In a mortar use a pestle to pound a piece of vanilla bean with an equal amount of sugar. This will extract the flavor. Add a cup or two of sugar, mix well, and put in an airtight container for use in desserts.

SUBSTITUTING INGREDIENTS IN RECIPES

FOR	USE
1 ounce unsweetened chocolate	3 tablespoons cocoa and 1 tablespoon vegetable shortening
1 cup honey	1¼ cups sugar and ¼ cup more liquid
1 cup whole milk	1 cup dry nonfat milk and 1½ teaspoons butter
1 cup sour milk	1 cup milk, fresh plus 1 tablespoon lemon juice or vinegar or ½ cup evaporated milk and ½ cup water plus 1 tablespoon lemon juice or vinegar. Let stand 5 minutes
1 cup sour milk	1 cup buttermilk
1 teaspoon baking powder	1 teaspoon baking soda and ½ cup sour milk
1 cup cake flour	1 cup all-purpose flour less 2 tablespoons

TIPS ON CAKE PANS

CAKE PANS may be heavy tin, aluminum or baking glass, and come in a variety of sizes. Most recipes call for an 8- or 9-inch square pan, 2 inches deep; or layer cake pans, either 8 or 9 inches across, and 1½ inches deep. A loaf cake pan is usually 8 x 4 inches, 3 inches deep. A tube, or angel-food pan, is usually 10 x 4 inches. Rectangular pans are available in a variety of sizes, a 13 x 9 x 2-inch being the most common. Bread pans may also be used for baking a loaf cake, and they are usually 9 x 5 x 3-inch, or 8 x 4 x 3-inch pans.

PIE PANS are measured across the top inside the rim. They come in 8-, 9-, or 10-inch sizes and are usually 1¼ inches deep.

COOKY SHEETS are made of medium-weight tin or aluminum. They are made without sides, and the 14 x 10 inch, or 15½ x 12 inch, are good sizes to have. The sheet should be small enough to allow the air to circulate around it in the oven.

CAKE RACKS are simple wire platforms which allow the cake or cookies to cook quickly. They prevent moisture from forming on the bottom of the cake or cookies.

CARE OF PANS. Don't use cake or pie pans for broiling. Don't run cold water onto a hot pan. Sudden changes of temperature will cause the pan to warp.

SUBSTITUTIONS OF CAKE PANS

If you haven't the size of cake pan specified in the recipe, you can substitute another size, remembering to fill the pan only half full, and to adjust the baking time. See p. 16.

Angel food, however, *must* be baked in a tube pan, and a pound cake in either a loaf or tube pan.

If a Cake Bakes As:	*It Will Also Bake As:*
2 8-inch layers	2 thin 8 x 8 x 2-inch squares 18 to 24 2½-inch cupcakes
3 8-inch layers	2 9 x 9 x 2-inch squares
2 9-inch layers	2 8 x 8 x 2-inch squares 3 thin 8-inch layers 1 15 x 10 x 1-inch rectangle 30 2½-inch cupcakes
1 8 x 8 x 2-inch square	1 9-inch layer
2 8 x 8 x 2-inch squares	2 9-inch layers 1 19 x 19 x 2-inch rectangle
1 9 x 9 x 1-inch square	2 thin 8-inch layers
2 9 x 9 x 2-inch squares	3 8-inch layers
1 19 x 9 x 2-inch rectangle	2 9-inch layers 2 8 x 8 x 2-inch squares
1 9 x 5 x 3-inch loaf pan	1 9 x 9 x 2-inch square 24 to 30 2½-inch cupcakes
1 9 x 3½-inch tube pan	2 9-inch layers 24 to 30 1½-inch cupcakes
1 10 x 4-inch tube pan	2 9 x 5 x 3-inch loaf pans 1 13 x 9 x 2-inch rectangle 2 15 x 10 x 1-inch rectangles

HOW MANY SERVINGS?

CAKES	SERVINGS
8-inch layer cake	will serve 10 to 14
9-inch layer cake	will serve 12 to 16
13 x 9 x 2-inch oblong cake	will serve 12 to 15
8- or 9-inch square cake	will serve 9
10-inch angel or chiffon cake	will serve 12 to 16

INSURING BAKING SUCCESS

PREPARATION OF THE PANS: This step, readying the pans in which you bake your cake, is important. Use an ungreased tube pan for angel food and sponge cakes. This applies to chiffon cakes as well. For other cakes the pans may be greased. For butter cakes I use butter, although many people say that an unsalted shortening is advisable as the butter may burn. I have not found this to be so, and prefer the flavor of the butter. After buttering, the pan should be lightly dusted with flour. I like cocoa for this when I am baking a chocolate cake. It looks and tastes better. Fill the pan about two-thirds full of batter and rap it sharply on the table once, to eliminate air holes.

BAKING TIPS. Stagger the pans in the oven, keeping them away from the oven wall, so that the heat can circulate evenly around them. If you are using only one pan, place it in the center of the oven.

A cake that is ready to come out of the oven will be springy when touched lightly in the center and will shrink away from the sides of the pan. You may test it by inserting a wooden pick in the center. If it comes out clean, the cake is done.

A cake comes out of a pan more easily if it is allowed to cool for 10 minutes or so in the pan. Angel food and spongecakes, however, should cool completely in the pan; invert the pan over a funnel or prop it up on both edges on cake racks or use some similar device.

Oven Temperatures

Very slow	250–275 degrees	Fahrenheit
Slow	300–325 ″	″
Moderate	350–375 ″	″
Moderately hot	400 ″	″
Hot	425 ″	″
Very hot	450–475 ″	″
Broil	500–525 ″	″

When baking a cake in a glass cake pan, lower the temperature 25° F.

All About Baking

GREASING AND FLOURING. Grease bottom and sides of pan generously, using approximately ½ tablespoon butter for each layer pan—a brush is convenient for greasing pans.

A better volume and appearance result from well-prepared pans.

A greased and floured pan gives the cake an almost crumb-free crust to make frosting the cake easier; it also locks in moisture.

CHECKING OVEN TEMPERATURE. Always preheat oven—baking directions are accurate only if oven is at recommended temperature.

Oven thermostats often fluctuate—have it checked periodically by your local utility company.

A portable oven thermometer is convenient to use to keep a check of oven temperature.

CHECKING DONENESS. Cake is done when:

It springs back when lightly touched with the finger.

It begins pulling away from the edges of the pan.

A wooden pick inserted in the center of the cake comes out clean.

Always test for doneness before removing cake from oven.

COOL. 10 or 15 minutes before removing from pan—warm cake is fragile; cooling gives strength necessary for handling.

If cake has cooled completely in the pan, rewarm bottom of pan a few seconds to remelt shortening.

Cool on a wire rack so that air can circulate freely.

Cool completely before frosting; most frostings will melt and will not adhere to a warm cake.

TIPS ON KEEPING CAKES

STORING CAKES UNTIL TIME TO SERVE. *Frosted cakes:* If frosted with a creamy frosting such as a fudge frosting or one made with confectioners' sugar, it can be kept at room temperature if covered well. Use a cake safe, or foil or plastic wrap. If the frosting is the fluffy type, made with egg whites, do not expect it to stand well. Cover with an inverted bowl or some similar protection, putting a spatula under the edge so that it is not airtight. If the cake is filled with a cream filling, or frosted with whipped cream, it should go in the refrigerator until serving time.

Unfrosted cakes: Be sure that these are cooled completely before wrapping and storing.

Freezing cakes. Cakes with creamy frosting: These freeze well and may be kept frozen for 2 to 3 months. Place them in a sturdy box and wrap the outside.

Cakes with a fluffy frosting: These should be frozen unwrapped to avoid injuring the frosting. As soon as the cake is frozen, wrap in plastic or foil wrap. A box will further protect the frosting. Wrap this as well. These may be kept for 2 or 3 months in the freezer.

Cakes frosted with whipped cream: This kind will also freeze well, but should not be held for more than 3 months before use.

Cakes with custard or fruit fillings: These do not freeze well as the cakes become soggy when thawed.

Cake batter: does not freeze satisfactorily as some of the leavening power is lost in the freezing.

Unfrosted cakes: Cool thoroughly before wrapping with foil or plastic and freezing. When freezing layers, place rounds of cardboard between them, and wrap as directed above.

Individual slices and also cupcakes may be wrapped and frozen.

THAWING FROZEN CAKES

Allow the cakes to stand at room temperature. Don't try to hurry the process by putting them in the oven.

Frosted cakes will take about 2 hours
Unfrosted layers will take about 1 hour
Cakes with whipped cream will take 3 to 4 hours in the refrigerator and are best thawed there
Cupcakes will take about 30 minutes
Individual slices will take about 5 minutes

TIPS ON FROSTING AND ICING CAKES

These are conveniently placed with the recipes for making the cake fillings, frostings, and icings.

BREADS

CHOCOLATE ALMOND COFFEE BREAD

Closely related to Swedish Tea Ring, but with something added, this might be made for that extra special breakfast.

1 envelope dry yeast	2 cups sifted flour
¼ cup warm water	½ cup seedless raisins
½ cup soft butter	½ cup chopped almonds
½ teaspoon salt	6 ounces semisweet choco-
¼ cup sugar	late, grated
1 egg	2 tablespoons dark rum
¼ cup lukewarm milk	Vanilla Icing I or II
	(p. 124)
	chopped almonds

1. Butter a baking sheet.

2. Dissolve the yeast in the warm water. Add half of the butter, the salt, and sugar, and stir to blend.

3. Beat the egg, add the milk, and stir into the yeast mixture. Add half of the flour and beat well. Add the remaining flour. Turn onto a floured board and knead until smooth.

4. Put in a buttered bowl, cover, and let rise until double in bulk. Punch down and let rise again.

5. Roll into an oblong; spread with the remaining soft butter. Sprinkle evenly with the raisins, nuts, and grated chocolate. Sprinkle the rum on top. Roll as for jelly roll, starting at the long edge. Place on the prepared baking sheet and seal the ends together to form a ring. Cut the ring with scissors every inch or so, cutting almost through it. Turn each slice so it lies flat with a cut side up.

6. Cover and let rise until double in bulk. Bake in a 375° F. oven for 20 to 25 minutes. Cool on a wire rack. Frost with vanilla icing and sprinkle additional chopped almonds on top.

CHOCOLATE COFFEE ROLL

This is a cross between a coffee cake and a cake. Serve it at any time of day with steaming cups of black coffee.

Cake

1 envelope dry yeast	1¼ cups sugar
¼ cup water	¼ teaspoon salt
2½ cups sifted flour	¼ cup butter
½ cup cocoa	3 eggs

1. Butter a cooky sheet.

2. Dissolve the yeast in the water.

3. Sift the flour, cocoa, sugar, and salt together. Cut in the butter with a pastry blender. Add the eggs, one at a time, beating well after each addition. Add the dissolved yeast and beat again. Put in a buttered bowl to rise for 2 hours, or until the dough has doubled.

4. In the meantime, make this filling:

Filling

2 ounces unsweetened chocolate (squares, melted, or envelopes)	½ cup honey
	2 cups filberts or hazelnuts, ground
2 tablespoons brandy	½ cup dried currants

1. Mix the filling ingredients thoroughly.

2. When the dough has risen, roll it out in an oblong about ½ inch thick. Spread with the filling, and roll like a jelly roll. Place on the cooky sheet. Bake in a 375° F. oven for 25 minutes and cool on a wire rack.

CHOCOLATE NUT BREAD

A wonderful cakelike bread to serve with tea or morning coffee. It keeps well, too.

3 cups biscuit mix	¼ cup honey
½ cup sugar	½ cup semisweet chocolate
1 egg	bits, chopped
¾ cup milk	½ cup chopped walnuts
½ cup orange juice	Confectioners' sugar, sifted
1 tablespoon grated orange	
rind	

1. Butter a 9-inch-square cake pan.

2. Mix the biscuit mix and the sugar in a bowl.

3. Beat the egg well; add the milk, orange juice, orange rind, and honey. Blend. Stir into the biscuit mix until well blended. Add the chocolate bits (I like to chop them in the blender first), and the nuts. Spread into the prepared pan.

4. Bake in a 350° F. oven for 55 to 60 minutes. Allow to cool for 10 minutes before turning out on a cake rack.

5. Dust with confectioners' sugar; or try Chocolate Frosting for Torten (p. 108) instead. Add some orange rind to the frosting to help it to blend perfectly with the bread.

CHOCOLATE TEA ROLLS

1 box (13½ ounces) hot	2 tablespoons butter
roll mix	½ teaspoon vanilla extract
4 ounces semisweet choco-	Confectioners' sugar, sifted
late	

1. Butter a 9-inch-square cake tin.

2. Melt the chocolate with the butter over hot water. Cool. Add the vanilla.

3. Follow the directions on the box of hot roll mix, allowing the dough to rise the first time. Roll out the risen dough to a rectangle about ¼ inch thick. Spread the cooled chocolate mixture evenly on top. Roll up as for a jelly roll. Cut into slices about ½ inch thick and place the slices in the pan, cut side up. Cover and let rise again until double in bulk.

4. Bake in a 375° F. oven for about 30 minutes. Remove from pan with a spatula, and sprinkle with confectioners' sugar. Cool on cake racks.

CINNAMON-CHOCOLATE COFFEE CAKE

A quickly prepared breakfast treat or midmorning snack. Serve with cups of steaming coffee.

1 box (10½ ounces) coffee cake mix	1 tablespoon grated orange rind
1 teaspoon ground cinnamon	2 squares semisweet chocolate, grated

Prepare coffee cake following directions on box. Add cinnamon, orange rind, and grated chocolate and mix. Bake as directed on the package.

GINGER CHOCOLATE HOLIDAY LOAF

These little loaves are full of spicy flavor. The dough may be made into rolls to be iced and served at breakfast or supper.

⅔ cup milk	2 tablespoons sugar
1¼ teaspoons salt	1 cup semisweet chocolate, put through a blender
6 tablespoons butter	
½ cup molasses	6 cups sifted flour
2 envelopes dry yeast	1 cup seedless raisins
⅔ cup lukewarm water	1 cup candied ginger, cut in small pieces
3 eggs	

1. Butter 2 loaf pans, 9 x 5 x 3 inches.

2. Scald the milk, and add salt, butter, and molasses. Stir to blend and cool to lukewarm.

3. Mix yeast and lukewarm water. Stir to dissolve the yeast, and add to molasses-milk mixture.

4. Beat the eggs, add the sugar and beat well. Stir this into the above mixture. Add the chocolate bits.

5. Sift a little of the flour over the raisins and ginger. Stir the remaining flour into the liquid mixture. Add the raisins and ginger.

6. Knead the dough on a floured board until smooth and elastic. Place in a buttered bowl, cover, and allow to rise until double in bulk, about 1½ hours.

7. Punch down the dough and knead again. Cut into halves and shape each half into a loaf. Put into the prepared pans, cover, and allow to rise again.

8. Bake in a 325° F. oven for 60 to 75 minutes, or until the loaves sound hollow when tapped and have begun to shrink from the sides of the pans.

HOLIDAY BREAD

This is a deliciously rich bread, and could well be served as a dessert with coffee, or at teatime.

6 eggs, separated	¾ cup ground almonds
¾ cup confectioners' sugar	½ cup confectioners' sugar
1 teaspoon vanilla extract	1 cup sifted flour
2 tablespoons dark rum	½ teaspoon salt
3 ounces unsweetened chocolate, grated	1 teaspoon grated nutmeg
	Rose Icing (p. 121)
¾ cup seedless raisins	Glacéed cherries and angelica
¾ cup mixed candied fruits	

1. Butter a 10-inch angel-food pan.

2. Beat the egg yolks until they are thick and lemon-colored. Beat in ¾ cup of the sugar gradually, then stir in the flavorings, the chocolate, raisins, candied fruits, and nuts.

3. Beat the egg whites until stiff, and then add the remaining ½ cup of sugar gradually. When the meringue is stiff, fold it carefully into the first mixture.

4. Sift the flour, salt, and nutmeg together and fold this, a little at a time, into the batter. Turn into the prepared pan.

5. Bake in a 325° F. oven for 50 to 60 minutes, or until the bread tests done with a wooden pick. Turn out to cool.

6. Ice with Rose Icing and decorate with glacéed cherries and angelica.

To serve, slice very thin.

FRUITED MOLASSES NUT BREAD

Molasses, orange, and chocolate combine to make this brimming-with-goodness loaf.

2⅔ cups sifted flour	½ cup orange juice
½ teaspoon baking soda	2 tablespoons salad oil
2 teaspoons baking powder	½ cup molasses
1½ teaspoons salt	1 cup broken walnut meats
½ cup sugar	3 ounces semisweet choco-
⅔ cup milk	late, grated
2 tablespoons grated	
orange rind	

1. Butter a loaf pan, 9 x 5 x 3 inches.

2. Sift the flour, baking soda, baking powder, and salt into a mixing bowl. Add the sugar.

3. Blend the milk, orange rind and juice, the oil, and molasses. Stir all at once into the dry ingredients. Add the nuts and chocolate. Do not overmix. Pour into the prepared pan.

4. Bake in a 325° F. oven for about 1¼ hours. Cool in the pan.

CAKES

I N MY OPINION, as well as that of practically everyone else, there is no more fitting crown to a festive occasion than a chocolate cake. By that I mean an honest chocolate cake—be it Fudge Layer Cake, Marble Chiffon, Red Devil's Food, or what-you-will. I mean a cake built from the finest ingredients: dark rich chocolate, fresh country eggs, sweet cream butter, mixed with loving care and a dash of eager anticipation.

Of course there are cakes you can whip up in a hurry from a package snatched from the grocer's shelf, and goodness knows these have a place in everyone's culinary program. But for that special occasion—Dad's birthday, Junior's class picnic, the day Sis entertains her sorority—a marvelous, memorable chocolate cake is the answer.

There are many kinds to choose from. In general there are four categories: *butter cakes*, which are made with butter or other shortening and use baking powder or soda as the leavening agent; *angel food and spongecakes*, which contain no shortening and rise because of the air whipped into the egg whites; *chiffon cakes*, which are made with oil and use both baking powder and egg whites as leavening agents; and finally, *raised cakes*, which use yeast to make them light and tender.

Perhaps you have a favorite recipe which does not include

chocolate in its list of ingredients. Will this not be enhanced by a creamy chocolate filling, or a dark, glossy chocolate icing?

Or, for a most important party, consider one of the wonderful *Torten* in the last section of this chapter.

In fact, your choice will delight everyone—it's chocolate!

BUTTER CAKES AND SOME WITH CREAM

A HONEY OF A CHOCOLATE CAKE

The honey gives this cake a special flavor, and the cake keeps well.

½ cup butter	2 teaspoons vanilla extract
¾ cup firmly packed brown sugar	2 cups sifted flour
	½ teaspoon salt
4 ounces unsweetened chocolate (envelopes or squares, melted and cooled)	1 teaspoon baking soda
	1 cup milk
	¾ cup honey
2 eggs	Black and White Peppermint Frosting (p. 104)

1. Butter two cake pans (8 x 8 x 2 inches) and dust with cocoa.

2. Cream the butter and brown sugar together. Add the chocolate; when thoroughly blended, add the eggs, one at a time, beating well after each addition. Add the vanilla and mix.

3. Sift the flour, salt, and baking soda together. Add to the butter mixture, alternating with the milk and honey which have been mixed together. Begin and end with the dry ingredients. Pour into the prepared pans.

4. Bake in a 375° F. oven for about 30 minutes, or until the cakes are springy in the center and shrink from the sides of the pans. Cool for 10 minutes.

5. Turn the cakes out of the pans and cool. Spread with Black and White Peppermint Frosting.

CHOCOLATE ALMOND CAKE

A delicate cake, fine in flavor and texture.

4 ounces unsweetened chocolate (squares, melted, or envelopes)

⅔ cup plus 3 tablespoons milk

1 egg yolk

1⅓ cups granulated sugar

2⅔ cups sifted flour

1 tablespoon baking powder

½ teaspoon baking soda

½ teaspoon salt

½ cup almonds

⅔ cup butter

¾ cup firmly packed brown sugar

1 tablespoon vanilla extract

4 whole eggs, separated

⅓ cup water

Coffee Rum and Butter Frosting (p. 114)

1. Butter a 9-inch-square pan and dust with cocoa.

2. Put the chocolate and ⅔ cup milk in the top of a double boiler and heat until they are well blended.

3. Stir the egg yolk and 1 cup of the granulated sugar together until well mixed. Add the hot chocolate-milk mixture slowly, stirring as your pour. Return to the double boiler and cook for a few minutes. Set aside to cool.

4. Sift the flour, baking powder, baking soda, and salt together.

5. Put the almonds in an electric blender for a few seconds, or chop finely.

6. Cream the butter and the brown sugar until light. Add the vanilla, then the 4 egg yolks, one at a time. Beat after each addition. Blend in the cooled chocolate mixture.

7. Mix the water and the 3 tablespoons of milk. Add the dry ingredients to the batter alternately with the milk and water. Add the nuts.

8. Whip the egg whites until stiff but not dry, and gradually beat in the remaining ⅓ cup granulated sugar. When rounded peaks are formed, fold the meringue gently into the batter. Pour the batter into the prepared cake pan.

9. Bake in a 375° F. oven for about 40 minutes, or until the cake is springy to the touch and shrinks from the sides of the pan.

10. Cool for 10 minutes and remove from pan. Frost when cold. Coffee Rum and Butter Frosting (p. 114) is perfect on this cake.

CHOCOLATE CARAMEL CAKE

½ cup butter
1¼ cups firmly packed brown sugar
1 teaspoon vanilla extract
2 eggs
3 ounces unsweetened chocolate (squares melted and cooled, or envelopes)

2 cups sifted flour
1½ teaspoons baking powder
½ teaspoon baking soda
½ teaspoon salt
1 cup milk
Caramel Frosting (p. 105)

1. Butter two 8-inch layer-cake pans and dust with cocoa.

2. Cream the butter with the brown sugar until light and fluffy. Add the vanilla. Add the eggs, one at a time, beating thoroughly after each addition. Then mix in the chocolate.

3. Sift together the flour, baking powder, baking soda, and salt. Add alternately with the milk, beginning and ending with the dry ingredients. Pour into the prepared pans.

4. Bake in a 350° F. oven for about 25 minutes, or until the cake is springy to the touch and shrinks from the sides of the pans.

5. Cool for 10 minutes, remove from pans and when cold, spread with Caramel Frosting.

CHOCOLATE CREAM-CHEESE CAKE

A soft fudgy cake that will please everyone.

3 tablespoons butter
1 package (3 ounces) cream cheese
1 cup sugar
2 eggs
1 teaspoon vanilla extract
3 ounces unsweetened choc-olate (squares, melted and cooled, or envelopes)
2 cups sifted flour
2 teaspoons baking powder
½ teaspoon salt
¾ cup milk
Chocolate Cream-Cheese Icing (p. 107)

1. Butter and dust with cocoa a 9-inch-square cake pan or a loaf pan (9 x 5 x 3 inches).

2. Cream the butter, the cheese, and the sugar until light and fluffy. Add the eggs, one at a time, beating after each addition. Stir in the vanilla. Beat in the cooled chocolate.

3. Sift the flour, baking powder, and salt together. Add to the cheese mixture alternately with the milk. Pour the batter into the prepared pan.

4. Bake in a 350° F. oven for about 60 minutes, or until the cake is springy in the center, and shrinks from the sides of the pan. Cool. Frost with Chocolate Cream-Cheese Icing.

CHOCOLATE HAZELNUT LAYER CAKE

This makes rather thin rich layers.

4 tablespoons dry bread crumbs
4 tablespoons bourbon
6 tablespoons butter
6 tablespoons granulated sugar
4 eggs, separated
2 ounces unsweetened choc-olate (squares, melted and cooled, or envelopes)
½ cup finely ground hazel-nuts
Pinch of salt
Hazelnut Filling (below)
Confectioners' sugar

1. Butter two 8-inch layer-cake pans.

2. Soak the bread crumbs in the bourbon.

3. Cream the butter and granulated sugar together until light and fluffy. Beat in the yolks, one at a time, beating after each addition. Beat in the chocolate, the soaked bread crumbs, and the nuts.

4. Whip the egg whites with the salt until stiff. Fold gently into the chocolate mixture. Spread the batter in the prepared pans.

5. Bake in a 325° F. oven for 30 minutes. Turn out on cake racks to cool. Put together with Hazelnut Filling. To serve, sift confectioners' sugar over the top. This cake is very good served in thin wedges with ice cream on the side. Be sure to pass chocolate sauce.

Hazelnut Filling

2 tablespoons soft butter	1 tablespoon heavy cream
½ cup confectioners' sugar	1 tablespoon bourbon
½ cup finely ground hazelnuts	

Mix all ingredients in a saucepan and place over low heat. Cook and stir until creamy and of the right consistency to spread. Put between cake layers.

CHOCOLATE MERINGUE DESSERT

Serve this cake without frosting for a not-too-sweet dessert; it is light and delicious.

Cake

½ cup butter	2 teaspoons vanilla extract
½ cup sugar	1 cup sifted flour
4 egg yolks	2 teaspoons baking powder
3 ounces unsweetened chocolate (squares, melted and cooled, or envelopes)	Pinch of salt
	6 tablespoons milk

1. Butter two 8-inch layer-cake pans and dust with cocoa.

2. Cream the butter and sugar together. Add the egg yolks, one at a time, beating well after each addition. Stir in the chocolate and the vanilla.

3. Sift the flour, baking powder, and a pinch of salt together and add to the chocolate mixture alternately with the milk. Pour into the prepared pans.

4. Make the meringue.

Meringue

4 egg whites
Salt
¾ cup sugar

1 teaspoon almond extract
½ cup chopped almonds

1. Whip the egg whites and salt until stiff but not dry. Add the sugar very gradually and beat until stiff peaks are formed. Add the almond flavoring.

2. Spread the meringue on the cake batter. Sprinkle with chopped almonds.

Bake in a 325° F. oven for 15 to 18 minutes. Remove from oven and cool.

3. Make the filling.

Filling

3 ounces chocolate (envelopes or squares)
3 tablespoons milk
1 cup confectioners' sugar

1 tablespoon cornstarch
1 teaspoon vanilla extract
Few grains of salt

1. Put chocolate and 2 tablespoons of the milk in the top of a double boiler and cook over simmering water until thoroughly blended. Stir in the sugar. Mix the cornstarch with 1 tablespoon of milk, and add to the chocolate mixture. Cook until the filling thickens, stirring while it cooks. Remove from the heat to cool. Add the flavoring and salt.

2. Spread the filling between the cooled layers of the cake.

CHOCOLATE MOLASSES CAKE

Chocolate and molasses are two flavors that can be combined delightfully.

2⅓ cups sifted flour
1½ teaspoons baking powder
½ teaspoon baking soda
½ teaspoon salt
½ teaspoon ground allspice
½ teaspoon ground cinnamon
½ cup firmly packed brown sugar

½ cup soft butter
¾ cup milk
2 eggs
1 cup molasses
2 ounces unsweetened chocolate (squares, melted and cooled, or envelopes)
Snowdrift Frosting (p. 123)
Walnuts, finely chopped

1. Butter cake pan (9 x 13 x 2 inches) and dust with cocoa.

2. Sift flour, baking powder, baking soda, salt, allspice, and cinnamon into the bowl of an electric mixer. Mix in the brown sugar. Add the soft butter and the milk, and beat until all ingredients are blended. Add the eggs, one at a time, beating after each addition. Then add the molasses and cooled chocolate. Pour into the prepared pan.

3. Bake in a 350° F. oven for about 35 minutes, or until the cake is springy to the touch and shrinks from the sides of the pan. This is good topped with Snowdrift Frosting and sprinkled with finely chopped walnuts.

CHOCOLATE SPICE CAKE

The applesauce in this recipe gives the cake wonderful keeping qualities, and also adds a delicious flavor that blends perfectly with the chocolate and spices.

2 cups sifted flour	4 tablespoons cocoa
1¼ cups sugar	1½ cups applesauce
2 teaspoons baking soda	½ cup milk
Pinch of salt	½ cup melted butter
½ teaspoon grated nutmeg	2 tablespoons dark rum
1 teaspoon ground cinnamon	1 cup raisins, chopped
	1 cup pecans, cut up
½ teaspoon ground allspice	Confectioners' sugar, sifted

1. Butter a cake pan (9 x 13 x 2 inches) and dust with cocoa.

2. Sift the flour, sugar, baking soda, salt, spices, and cocoa together. Stir in the applesauce, milk, butter, and rum. Mix thoroughly. Add the raisins and nuts. Spread in the prepared pan.

3. Bake in a 350° F. oven for 45 minutes, or until the cake springs back to the touch and shrinks away from the sides of the pan. Cool for 10 minutes. Turn out on a cake rack to cool completely. Dust with confectioners' sugar.

CHOCOLATE SUNDAE CAKE

This is a simple cake with its own sauce.

1. Butter a 9-inch-square baking pan and dust with cocoa.

2. Make the sauce next.

Sauce

1 cup sugar	1 teaspoon cornstarch
4 tablespoons cocoa	¼ cup milk
	2 tablespoons butter

1. Mix the sugar, cocoa, and cornstarch together. Stir in the milk.

Cook and stir until hot and smooth. Add the butter, mix, and pour the sauce into the prepared pan.

2. Make the batter.

Batter

2 cups sifted flour	1 teaspoon vanilla extract
2½ teaspoons baking pow- der	1 egg
1 teaspoon salt	1 cup milk
1 cup sugar	2 ounces chocolate
⅓ cup soft butter	(squares, melted, or en- velopes)

1. Sift the flour, baking powder, salt, and sugar into a mixing bowl. Add the butter, vanilla, egg, and milk. Stir in the chocolate and beat all for 2 minutes. Pour the batter into the pan, over the sauce, spreading evenly.

2. Bake in a 350° F. oven for 40 to 45 minutes, or until the cake is springy to the touch. Turn out onto a serving dish. Cut into squares. To serve, you may top with whipped cream if you wish.

CINNAMON CAKE WITH COCOA ICING

Since cinnamon ice cream with hot fudge sauce is a favorite, why not a cinnamon cake? Here it is. The cinnamon is very delicate and the icing should be one that is not too chocolatey.

½ cup butter	1½ teaspoons baking pow- der
1 cup sugar	
2 eggs, separated	3 teaspoons ground cinna- mon
¼ teaspoon red food color- ing	1 cup milk
1½ cups sifted flour	Pinch of salt
	Cocoa Icing (p. 113)

1. Butter a 9-inch-square cake pan and dust with cocoa.

2. Cream the butter and sugar together well. Beat in the egg yolks, one at a time. Then blend in the food coloring. If you like a very pink cake, add a little more.

3. Sift the dry ingredients together and add to the first mixture alternately with the milk.

4. Beat the egg whites with the salt until stiff but not dry. Fold gently into batter. Pour into the prepared pan.

5. Bake in a 350° F. oven for 25 minutes, or until the cake is springy to the touch and shrinks away from the sides of the pan. Turn out. When cold, frost with Cocoa Icing.

COCOA CUPCAKES

½ cup butter	1½ cups sifted flour
1½ cups sugar	3 teaspoons baking powder
3 eggs	½ teaspoon salt
¾ cup cocoa	⅔ cup milk
1 teaspoon ground cinnamon	1 teaspoon vanilla extract
	Caramel Frosting (p. 105)

1. Butter two cupcake pans (each making 8 average-size cupcakes) and dust with cocoa.

2. Cream the butter and sugar well. Add the eggs, one at a time, beating after each addition.

3. Sift the cocoa, cinnamon, flour, baking powder, and salt together. Add to the creamed mixture a little at a time, alternating with the milk. Stir in the vanilla. Spoon into the prepared tins, filling them about two-thirds full.

4. Bake in a 375° F. oven for 30 minutes, or until the cakes are springy to the touch and shrink away from the sides of the pans. Frost when cold with Caramel Frosting.

Variations: CHOCOLATE SUNDAE CUPCAKES

Cut cupcakes horizontally into halves. Put a small scoop of ice cream on the lower half. Replace the top and pour your choice of Chocolate Sauces (pp. 199 ff.) on top.

Remove the center of the top of each cake. Fill the hollows with raspberry jam, replace the top, and frost with Chocolate Butter Icing (pp. 106–107)

COCOA FRUITCAKE

This recipe comes from the West Indies, and is well worth trying.

½ cup butter
1 cup sugar
3 eggs
2 cups sifted flour
1 tablespoon baking powder

1 teaspoon salt
¼ cup cocoa
2½ cups crystallized fruit
¾ cup milk
Almond Paste Icing (p. 103)

1. Butter a loaf pan (9 x 5 x 3 inches) and dust with cocoa.

2. Cream the butter and sugar well. Add the eggs, one at a time, beating after each addition.

3. Sift the flour, baking powder, salt, and cocoa together. Shake a little over the crystallized fruit. Add the dry ingredients to the batter, a little at a time, alternately with the milk. Fold in the fruit. Pour into the prepared pan.

4. Bake in a 350° F. oven for about 1 hour, or until a wooden pick inserted in the center comes out clean. Almond Paste Icing is a wonderful topping for this delicious cake.

COUNTRY FAIR CAKE

Its old-fashioned goodness is hard to beat.

2 cups semisweet chocolate bits	½ teaspoon baking soda
½ cup butter	1 teaspoon baking powder
1 cup sugar	1 teaspoon salt
2 eggs	1 cup milk
2 cups sifted flour	Rich Chocolate Frosting (p. 120)

1. Butter an 8-inch cake pan and dust with cocoa.

2. Melt the chocolate bits over hot water and set aside to cool.

3. Cream the butter and add the sugar gradually. Add the eggs, one at a time, beating after each addition.

4. Sift the dry ingredients together. Add these alternately with the milk, beginning and ending with the flour mixture. Stir in the melted and cooled chocolate. Pour into the prepared pan.

5. Bake in a 350° F. oven for 25 minutes, or until the cake is springy to the touch and has shrunk from the sides of the pan. When cool, frost with Rich Chocolate Frosting.

Note: If you prefer a layer cake, use two 9-inch pans, and bake for 20 minutes only.

DARK CHOCOLATE FRUITCAKE

If you are fond of fruitcake, and who isn't, you will enjoy serving this on festive occasions. I use candied fruit prepared for fruit-cake, but you may substitute dates and figs if you like.

1½ cups candied fruit	4 ounces unsweetened chocolate (squares, melted and cooled, or envelopes)
1 cup seedless raisins	
½ cup brandy	
¾ cup butter	2 cups sifted flour
1½ cups sugar	1 teaspoon baking powder
6 eggs, separated	1½ cups pecans, coarsely chopped

1. Put the fruit in a bowl and pour the brandy over it. Let this stand overnight. Drain the fruit, reserving the brandy.

2. Butter 2 loaf pans (9 x 5 x 3 inches) generously.

3. Cream the butter, adding 1 cup of the sugar gradually. Beat in the egg yolks, two at a time, beating after each addition. Stir in the cooled chocolate.

4. Sift the flour and baking powder together and add to the batter, alternating with the reserved brandy. (Here, if the fruit has absorbed most of the brandy, it does no harm to add a little more.) Stir in the fruit and the nuts.

5. Beat the egg whites until fairly stiff, and add the remaining ½ cup sugar slowly, beating until the mixture stands in soft peaks. Fold this into the batter, and spoon into the prepared pans.

6. Bake in a 250° F. oven for 2 hours. When a wooden pick inserted is dry when it is withdrawn, the cake is done. Cool.

7. Remove from the pans. Pour a few tablespoonfuls of brandy over each cake and wrap in foil. Store for 6 or 8 weeks. During this time, sprinkle with brandy two or three times. Serve any time thereafter.

FAVORITE LOAF CAKE

This is a light and luscious cake, which we just slice and serve as it is. Served with a fruit ice or sherbet, it makes a perfect summer dessert.

¾ cup butter
2 cups sugar
3 ounces unsweetened chocolate (squares melted, or envelopes)
4 eggs, separated

1¾ cups sifted flour
½ teaspoon salt
1 teaspoon baking powder
1 cup milk
1 teaspoon vanilla extract

1. Butter a loaf pan (9 x 5 x 3) and dust with cocoa.

2. Cream the butter and sugar together until light and fluffy.

Stir in the chocolate, and the egg yolks, one at a time, beating after each addition.

3. Sift the flour, salt, and baking powder together, and add about one third to the batter. Beat in half of the milk. Continue alternating the milk and the dry ingredients until all are used. Add the vanilla.

4. Beat the egg whites until stiff and fold these into the batter. Pour into the prepared pan.

5. Bake in a 350° F. oven for about 45 minutes, or until the cake is springy to the touch and shrinks away from the sides of the pan.

FRENCH CHOCOLATE CAKE

This is cake with a delicate chocolate touch, not too rich, but light as a feather.

¾ cup boiling water	1 teaspoon vanilla extract
½ cup cocoa	2 cups sifted flour
½ teaspoon baking soda	¼ teaspoon salt
½ cup sour cream	3 egg whites
½ cup butter	French Frosting (p. 117)
2 cups sugar	

1. Butter 2 layer-cake pans and dust with flour.

2. Pour the boiling water on the cocoa and stir to make a paste. Cool. Mix the baking soda and sour cream.

3. Cream the butter and sugar. Beat in the cocoa mixture, the vanilla, and the soda and sour cream mixture. Slowly add the flour and salt. Beat all together thoroughly.

4. Whip the egg whites until stiff but not dry. Fold gently into the batter and turn into the prepared pans.

5. Bake in a 350° F. oven for about 20 minutes, or until the cake is springy to the touch and shrinks from the sides of the pans. Turn out on racks to cool. Frost with French Frosting.

FUDGE LAYER CAKE

5 ounces unsweetened chocolate (squares, melted, or
envelopes)
½ cup hot water
1¾ cups sugar
½ cup butter
3 eggs
2 cups sifted flour

1 teaspoon baking soda
1 teaspoon salt
⅔ cup milk
1 tablespoon vanilla ex-
tract
Fudge Frosting (p. 117)
1 cup chopped toasted al-
monds

1. Butter 3 layer-cake pans and dust with cocoa.

2. Blend chocolate and hot water over low heat. Add ½ cup of
the sugar and stir and cook for a minute or two. Cool.

3. Cream the butter with the remaining 1¼ cups sugar. Beat in
the eggs, one at a time. Add the chocolate mixture.

4. Sift the flour, baking soda, and salt together and add alternately with the milk. Stir in the vanilla. Pour the batter into the
prepared pans.

5. Bake in a 350° F. oven for 20 to 25 minutes, or until the layers are springy to the touch in the center. Allow to stand for 10
minutes, and then turn out on wire cake racks.

6. When cold, fill and frost with Fudge Frosting and press the
chopped almonds onto the sides of the cake.

GINGER CHOCOLATE CAKE

*This is an unusual combination of flavors, which you will find
intriguing. The method of mixing is different, and quick, too.*

2 cups sifted flour
1½ cups granulated sugar
½ cup cocoa
1 tablespoon baking pow-
der
1 teaspoon salt
½ teaspoon ground ginger

1 cup soft butter
1½ cups milk
1 tablespoon molasses
1 teaspoon vanilla extract
2 eggs
Chocolate Orange Frosting
(p. 110)

1. Butter a cake pan (13 x 9 x 2 inches) and dust with cocoa.

2. Sift dry ingredients together into the large bowl of an electric mixer. Add the butter and 1 cup of the milk. Beat for 2 minutes on medium speed. Now add the rest of the milk, the molasses, vanilla, and eggs. Beat for 2 minutes more. Pour into the prepared pan

3. Bake in a 350° F. oven for 35 to 40 minutes, or until the cake s springy to the touch and shrinks from the sides of the pan. Cool for 10 minutes. Remove from the pan and, when cold, frost with Chocolate Orange Frosting.

Variation: Try slicing this cake horizontally and filling it with Wine Custard Filling (p. 101).

GRANDMOTHER'S CHOCOLATE PECAN CAKE

This old-fashioned cake is a universal favorite. Not too rich, but delicious in flavor.

½ cup butter	2 teaspoons baking powder
1½ cups sugar	⅛ teaspoon salt
2 eggs	1 cup milk
1 teaspoon vanilla extract	1 cup broken pecan meats
2 cups sifted flour	Chocolate Butter Icing
3 tablespoons cocoa	(pp. 106–107)

1. Butter 2 layer-cake pans and dust with cocoa.

2. Cream the butter and sugar together until light and fluffy. Add the eggs, one at a time, beating after each addition. Add the vanilla.

3. Sift the dry ingredients together and add alternately with the milk. Stir in half of the nuts and pour the batter into the prepared pans.

4. Bake in a 350° F. oven for 30 to 40 minutes, or until the cake is springy in the center and shrinks from the sides of the pans.

5. Cool the layers, put together, and frost with Chocolate Butter Icing. Sprinkle the top with the remaining nuts, chopped fine.

HAZELNUT BUTTER CAKE

A fine butter cake is the foundation of many a French pastry dessert. It is well worth the trouble, and will make your reputation as a cook.

4 eggs, separated
10 tablespoons sugar
1 cup sifted flour
⅓ cup butter, melted and cooled

¾ cup finely ground hazelnuts
Chocolate Pastry Cream I (pp. 96–97)
Chocolate Curls (p. 126)

1. Butter a 9-inch round 2-inch deep cake pan and sprinkle it with flour.

2. Beat the egg yolks until they are light and add the sugar gradually, beating until the mixture ribbons. Sift a little flour at a time over this, folding each addition in gently.

3. Beat the egg whites until stiff. Carefully fold them into the batter. Fold in the cooled butter, pouring off the top, and discarding the sediment at the bottom. Finally, fold in ½ cup of the nuts.

4. Bake in a 350° F. oven for 40 minutes, or until the cake is springy to the touch in the center. Turn out onto a cake rack.

To serve: When completely cold, split into 2 layers and fill and frost with Chocolate Pastry Cream I. Shake the rest of the hazelnuts on top of the cake, and add a wreath of Chocolate Curls (p. 126) around the edge.

HONEY CINNAMON CAKE

¼ cup butter
½ cup sugar
½ cup honey
1 egg
1¼ cups sifted flour
1 teaspoon baking soda

2 teaspoons ground cinnamon
½ teaspoon salt
½ cup water
Rich Chocolate Frosting (p. 120)

1. Butter a 9-inch-square cake pan and dust it with cocoa.

2. Cream the butter and sugar together well. Add the honey and beat well again. Then beat in the egg.

3. Sift the dry ingredients together, and add to the batter alternately with the water. Turn into the prepared pan.

4. Bake in a 350° F. oven for 25 to 30 minutes, or until the cake comes away from the sides of the pan and is springy to the touch.

Use a chocolate frosting, such as Rich Chocolate Frosting or serve with chocolate ice cream or vanilla ice cream with chocolate sauce.

MAHOGANY CAKE

This is a beautiful dark cake which has coffee as its liquid ingredient.

1½ cups butter	1½ cups sifted flour
1¼ cups sugar	½ teaspoon salt
3 eggs	1 teaspoon baking powder
2 ounces unsweetened chocolate (squares, cut up, or envelopes)	1 teaspoon baking soda
	2 teaspoons vanilla extract
	Mocha Frosting (p. 119)
1 cup very strong hot coffee	or Fluffy Cocoa Frosting (p. 116)

1. Butter two 8-inch layer-cake pans.

2. Cream the butter and sugar together until light and fluffy. Add the eggs, one at a time, beating after each addition.

3. Blend the chocolate and the hot coffee, stirring until the chocolate is melted.

4. Sift the dry ingredients together, and add to the butter mixture, alternating with the coffee-chocolate mixture. Add the vanilla. Spread in the prepared pans.

5. Bake in a 350° F. oven for about 30 minutes, or until the cake springs back when touched lightly in the center, and has begun to shrink from the sides of the pans. Turn out on cake racks and cool. Put layers together with Mocha Frosting or Fluffy Cocoa Frosting.

MANITOU BLACK CAKE

For this excellent recipe we are indebted to our Canadian neighbors. It is a rich moist cake, and utterly delicious.

¼ cup butter
1 cup sugar
1 egg
1 tablespoon vanilla extract
3 ounces unsweetened chocolate (squares, melted and cooled, or envelopes)

1½ cups sifted flour
2 teaspoons baking powder
1 teaspoon baking soda
½ teaspoon salt
1½ cups milk
Sherry Icing (p. 122)

1. Butter a 9-inch-square cake pan and dust with cocoa.

2. Cream the butter with the sugar. Add the egg and beat well. Stir in the vanilla, then the chocolate.

3. Sift the flour, baking powder, baking soda, and salt together. Beat this in, a little at a time, alternating with the milk. Pour into the prepared pan.

4. Bake in a 375° F. oven for 50 minutes, or until the cake is springy to the touch and shrinks from the sides of the pan. Turn out and cool.

Sherry Icing is perfect with this cake.

MOCHA MARBLE CAKE

This starts with a fine butter cake, as do many delectable French pastries.

4 eggs, separated
10 tablespoons sugar
1 cup sifted flour
½ cup butter, melted and cooled
2 tablespoons cocoa

1 teaspoon instant coffee powder
Chocolate Butter Icing (pp. 106–107)
¾ cup walnuts, ground finely or grated in a blender

1. Butter a round 8 x 2 inch deep cake pan and dust it with flour.

2. Beat the egg yolks until light. Add the sugar very slowly, continuing to beat until the mixture is thick and creamy. Sift the flour over this, a little at a time, and fold it in gently as you sift.

3. Beat the egg whites until stiff, and fold these in carefully also. Then fold in the butter, using just the liquid on the top, and discarding the sediment at the bottom. Spread half of this batter in the prepared pan.

4. Add the cocoa and coffee powder to the rest of the batter and mix. Spoon on top of the plain batter. With a spatula, swirl the chocolate part around so as to mix slightly.

5. Bake in a 350° F. oven for 40 minutes, or until the cake is springy to the touch in the center. Turn out on a cake rack.

6. When completely cold, split and fill with Chocolate Butter Icing. Spread this on the top also, and cover with the ground walnuts.

MOCHA RAISIN CAKE

This recipe was given to me by a friend whose grandmother brought it from the old country. She has adjusted it to suit the ingredients available here, and the result is a delicious chocolatey-spicy cake. Adding an icing is like gilding the lily, but do it if you like.

2 cups boiling water	3 tablespoons cocoa
2 heaping teaspoons instant coffee powder	½ teaspoon baking soda
	2 teaspoons baking powder
2 cups granulated sugar	½ teaspoon salt
1 cup seedless raisins, chopped	1 teaspoon ground cinnamon
½ cup butter	1 teaspoon ground nutmeg
1 teaspoon vanilla extract	½ teaspoon ground cloves
2 eggs	½ teaspoon ground allspice
2 cups sifted flour	Confectioners' sugar, sifted

1. Butter a 10-inch-square cake pan and dust it with cocoa.

2. Pour the boiling water on the instant coffee powder. Add 1 cup of the granulated sugar and chopped raisins. Simmer this over low heat for 10 minutes. Set aside to cool.

3. Cream the butter with the second cup of granulated sugar until it is light and fluffy. Add the vanilla, and the eggs, one at a time, beating well after each addition.

4. Sift the flour, cocoa, baking soda, baking powder, salt, and spices together. It may seem like an overabundance of spices, but don't skimp. Beat a little into the creamed mixture, then add a little of the coffee mixture. Repeat until all is used. Pour the batter into the prepared pan.

5. Bake in a 350° F. oven for about 60 minutes, or until the cake is springy to the touch and shrinks away from the sides of the pan. When cool, turn out, and dust the top with confectioners' sugar.

OLD-TIME CURRANT CAKE

This old-fashioned treat used to be served in the afternoon with a glass of homemade wine.

1 cup butter	½ teaspoon ground mace
1 cup sugar	½ cup currants
1 egg, whole	1 teaspoon crushed carda-
3 eggs, separated	mom seeds
2 cups sifted flour	2 tablespoons brandy
Pinch of salt	Creamy Chocolate Frosting
	(p. 115)

1. Butter a baking pan, 13 x 9 x 2 inches

2. Cream the butter and sugar together until light and fluffy. Beat in the whole egg and 3 egg yolks, one at a time, beating after each addition.

3. Beat the 3 egg whites stiff.

4. Sift the flour, salt, and mace together. Shake a little over the currants. Add the flour mixture to the batter a little at a time, alternating with the beaten egg whites. Fold in the currants, the cardamom seeds, and the brandy. Spread the batter in the prepared pan.

5. Bake in a 350° F. oven for about 45 minutes, or until the cake springs back when touched lightly in the center. Turn out on a cake rack to cool. Frost with Creamy Chocolate Frosting.

ORANGE CAKE WITH CHOCOLATE FROSTING

Here again is that delightful combination of orange and chocolate flavors. If you care to make it even more orangy, spread a little orange marmalade on the cake before icing it.

¾ cup butter	¾ teaspoon salt
1½ cups sugar	½ cup orange juice
Grated rind of 1 orange	2 tablespoons lemon juice
3 eggs	1 tablespoon dark rum
3 cups sifted flour	½ cup water
3½ teaspoons baking powder	Glossy Chocolate Frosting (p. 118), double recipe

1. Prepare three 8-inch layer-cake pans by buttering them and dusting them with flour.

2. Cream the butter with the sugar until light and fluffy. Add the orange rind, and then the eggs, one at a time, beating well after each addition.

3. Sift the flour, baking powder, and salt together, and add this, a little at a time, alternating with the mixed liquids. Pour into the prepared pans.

4. Bake in a 375° F. oven for 30 minutes, or until the cake is springy to the touch and shrinks from the sides of the pans. Cool for 10 minutes in the pans, then turn out on cake racks. When cold, put layers together and ice with Glossy Chocolate Frosting, using double the recipe given.

RED DEVIL'S FOOD

You will find this a family favorite. The method of mixing this cake is different, but the good chocolate flavor is there.

2 cups sifted flour
1½ cups sugar
¾ teaspoon salt
½ cup soft butter
2 eggs
1 cup milk
1 teaspoon vanilla extract
1 teaspoon red food coloring

2½ ounces chocolate (squares, melted and cooled, or envelopes)
1 teaspoon baking soda
1 tablespoon hot water
½ cup semisweet chocolate bits

1. Butter a 9-inch-square cake pan and dust it with cocoa.

2. Sift the flour, sugar, and salt into the bowl of an electric mixer. Add the soft butter, the eggs, and ½ cup of the milk, all at once. Beat at low speed for 2 minutes.

3. Blend the remaining milk, the vanilla, food coloring, chocolate, baking soda, and hot water. Add to the rest, and beat for another 2 minutes. Pour into the prepared cake pan. Sprinkle with the chocolate bits.

4. Bake in a 350° F. oven for 25 to 30 minutes, or until the cake is springy in the center and shrinks from the sides of the pan. We like this cake without frosting, but you may omit the chocolate bits and frost with the icing of your choice.

SEMISWEET CHOCOLATE CAKE

Light as a cloud; not too rich.

8 ounces (squares) semisweet chocolate
¼ cup water
¾ cup butter
¾ cup sugar

1⅓ cups sifted flour
1 tablespoon vanilla extract
8 egg whites
Pinch of salt

1. Butter two cake pans (13 x 9 x 2 inches) and dust with cocoa.

2. Put the chocolate and the water in the top of a double boiler and heat over simmering water until the two are well blended. Cool.

3. Cream the butter and sugar together until fluffy. Beat in the flour alternately with the chocolate mixture. Add the vanilla.

4. Whip the egg whites with the salt until they are stiff. Fold them gently into the batter. Spread in the prepared pans.

5. Bake in a 350° F. oven for 30 to 35 minutes, or until the cake is springy to the touch and shrinks from the sides of the pans.

We like to serve this with a scoop of ice cream on top, and perhaps chocolate sauce over that.

POUNDCAKE

This makes 2 cakes. Cut the recipe into halves to use in the following recipes.

2 cups butter	½ teaspoon freshly grated
2 cups sugar	nutmeg
9 eggs	1¾ cups sifted flour
2 tablespoons bourbon	½ teaspoon cream of tartar
2 teaspoons vanilla extract	½ teaspoon salt

1. Prepare two loaf pans (9 x 5 x 3 inches); butter them, then line with wax paper, and butter the paper.

2. Cream the butter and sugar, adding the sugar gradually. Add the eggs, one at a time, beating after each addition. Add the bourbon, vanilla, and nutmeg.

3. Sift the flour, cream of tartar, and salt together, and add slowly to the batter. Pour into the prepared pans.

4. Bake in a 325° F. oven for 60 minutes, or until a wooden pick inserted in the cakes is dry when removed.

CHOKAULU CAKE

1 Poundcake (p. 54)
Chokaulu liqueur

2 cups heavy cream, whipped
Glacéed cherries
Almonds

1. Slice poundcake into 4 horizontal layers. Sprinkle liberally with the liqueur and allow to stand.

2. Put together with whipped cream between the layers and on top and sides. Decorate with glacéed cherries and halved almonds.

CHOCOLATE RASPBERRY DESSERT

This is a wonderful dessert with an intriguing combination of flavors.

5 egg yolks
5 teaspoons sugar
3 tablespoons dark rum

1 cup heavy cream
1 Poundcake (p. 54)
Seedless raspberry jam
Bittersweet Chocolate Frosting (p. 104)

1. Beat egg yolks and sugar together until light and creamy. Add the rum.

2. Whip the cream and fold into the first mixture.

3. Slice the cake into 3 or 4 horizontal layers. Spread the lower layers with the jam and then with the rum cream.

4. Spread Bittersweet Chocolate Frosting on the top. Chill for several hours before serving.

RICH CREAM CAKE

This is an Italian specialty, tempting and delicious.

4 tablespoons cornstarch
3 cups milk
4 eggs, beaten
3 tablespoons sugar
1 tablespoon butter
1 teaspoon almond extract

1 teaspoon vanilla extract
1 Poundcake (p. 54)
2 ounces semisweet chocolate, grated
6 candied cherries, chopped

1. Mix the cornstarch with ½ cup of the milk. Add the rest of the milk, the beaten eggs, and the sugar and cook over low heat until the mixture comes to a boil, stirring as it cooks. Add butter, cool, and then add the flavorings.

2. Slice the cake into very thin horizontal layers, and put them together with the cold custard, spreading it on top as well. Chill for several hours. Decorate the top with the grated chocolate and cherries just before serving.

COCOA CREAM CAKE

This cake has cream as its main ingredient instead of the more usual butter. It is light and delicate.

1 cup heavy cream
2 eggs
2 teaspoons vanilla extract
1½ cups sifted flour

1 cup sugar
½ cup cocoa
2 teaspoons baking powder
½ teaspoon salt

1. Butter a loaf pan (9 x 5 x 3 inches) and dust with cocoa.

2. Whip the cream until it is stiff. Beat in the eggs, one at a time, and the vanilla.

3. Sift the flour, sugar, cocoa, baking powder, and salt together. Sift gradually over the batter, folding as you sift. Pour into the prepared pan.

4. Bake in a 350° F. oven for 50 to 60 minutes, or until the cake is springy to the touch and shrinks from the sides of the pan. Remove to a cake rack, and after 10 minutes turn the cake out to cool.

Serve this with sherbet or ice cream, or use it as a base for any dessert, preferably one topped with chocolate sauce.

MOCHA CREAM CAKE

A luscious light dessert, worthy of being served to your most important guests.

2 eggs	1 teaspoon instant coffee
1 cup granulated sugar	powder
¼ teaspoon salt	1 teaspoon baking powder
1 teaspoon vanilla extract	2 cups heavy cream
1 tablespoon butter	1 tablespoon dark rum
½ cup milk	2 tablespoons confection-
1 cup sifted flour	ers' sugar
3 tablespoons cocoa	

1. Butter three 8-inch layer-cake pans and dust them with cocoa.

2. Beat the eggs until they are thick and lemon-colored. Add the granulated sugar, salt, and vanilla.

3. Bring the butter and milk to the boiling point. Beat slowly into the egg mixture.

4. Sift the flour, cocoa, coffee powder, and baking powder together. Add to the liquid and beat well. Pour into the cake pans.

5. Bake in a 350° F. oven until the cake shrinks from the sides of the pans. This should take about 25 minutes. Cool and turn out.

6. Whip the cream until stiff, add rum and confectioners' sugar, and spread between the layers and on top of the cake. Chill well before serving.

Makes 10 to 12 servings.

BOSTON CREAM PIE

Actually, this is a cake with creamy filling. This will make 2 cakes with rather thin layers. Split the two, to make a 4-layer cake.

Cake

3 eggs
1 cup sugar
1½ cups sifted flour

2 teaspoons baking powder
3 tablespoons water
Glossy Chocolate Frosting (p. 118)

1. Butter two 9-inch layer-cake pans and dust them with flour.

2. Beat the eggs until thick and lemon-colored. Spoon the sugar in slowly and continue beating until light.

3. Sift the flour and baking powder together and fold gently into the egg-sugar mixture. Last, stir in the water. Pour into the prepared pans.

4. Bake in a 350° F. oven for about 20 to 25 minutes, or until the cakes are springy to the touch and shrink from the sides of the pans. Turn out on a cake rack to cool.

Filling

½ cup sugar
Pinch of salt
4 tablespoons flour
2 eggs

2 cups milk, scalded
2 tablespoons butter
1 teaspoon vanilla extract

1. Mix the sugar, salt and flour in the top of a double boiler. Beat the eggs well and add. Mix thoroughly and pour in the hot milk slowly, stirring as you pour. Stir and cook over simmering water until the filling is thick and smooth. Allow to cook for 10 minutes more, stirring occasionally. Add butter. Add vanilla. Cool.

2. Split each cake into layers, and spread three layers with the filling, putting them together as you spread. Frost the top layer with Glossy Chocolate Frosting, allowing it to drip down the sides of the cake.

Makes 10 to 12 servings.

CHOCOLATE WALNUT CAKE

A tempting teatime treat.

9 eggs, separated
2 cups granulated sugar
4 ounces chocolate
    (squares, melted and
    cooled, or envelopes)

2 tablespoons brandy
3 cups sifted flour
2 cups ground walnuts
Confectioners' sugar, sifted

1. Butter a cake pan (12 x 8 x 2 inches) and dust with cocoa.

2. Beat the egg yolks with the granulated sugar until thick and lemon-colored. Add the chocolate and the brandy. Blend.

3. Beat the egg whites until stiff but not dry. Fold them into the first mixture.

4. Sift the flour over the batter in small amounts, folding in gently. Fold in the nuts.

5. Bake in a 325° F. oven for 30 minutes. Cool and turn out of the pan. Dust with confectioners' sugar. Cut into squares. Serve with fruit or ice cream.

ANGEL FOOD AND SPONGECAKE

COCOA ANGEL FOOD

When you make this heavenly cake, remember that the egg whites should be at room temperature before you whip them, to produce this cake of incredible lightness.

1½ cups egg whites
    (about 12)
½ teaspoon salt
1 teaspoon cream of tartar
1¼ cups sugar

2 teaspoons vanilla extract
¾ cup sifted flour
½ cup cocoa
Fluffy Walnut Icing
    (pp. 116–117)

1. Beat the egg whites until they are frothy. Add the salt and cream of tartar, then ¾ cup of the sugar, very gradually. Continue to beat until soft peaks are formed. Add the vanilla.

2. Sift the flour, the remaining ½ cup of sugar, and the cocoa together. Sift this, a little at a time, over the egg-white mixture, folding it in gently. Pour the batter into an ungreased 10-inch angel-cake pan. Cut through in several places with a spatula to remove air bubbles.

3. Bake in a 350° F. oven for 45 minutes, or until the cake is springy to the touch. Invert until the cake is cold.

4. Remove from the pan and frost with Fluffy Walnut Icing.

COCOA SPONGECAKE

5 eggs, separated	¾ cup plus 2 tablespoons
1 cup sugar	sifted flour
2 tablespoons orange juice	4 tablespoons cocoa
1 teaspoon grated orange rind	Pinch of salt
1 teaspoon vanilla extract	Chocolate Orange Frosting (p. 110)

1. Beat the egg yolks, add ½ cup of the sugar, orange juice, rind, and vanilla. Beat until very thick and light.

2. Sift flour and cocoa together.

3. Beat egg whites and salt until slightly stiff. Add the remaining ½ cup of sugar slowly, beating as you add. Beat until soft peaks are formed. Gently fold in the egg-yolk mixture, then the flour and cocoa, a little at a time. Pour the batter into an ungreased 9- or 10-inch angel-cake pan.

4. Bake in a 325° F. oven for 1 hour. Turn upside down over a funnel until the cake is cold.

5. Remove from the pan and frost with Chocolate Orange Frosting.

CREAM-CHEESE TART WITH FRUIT

The Italians, whose "tart" this is, have an intriguing way of combining cheese and chocolate.

1½ pounds ricotta (Italian cottage cheese)
½ cup sugar
2 ounces semisweet chocolate, grated
2 teaspoons almond extract
1 spongecake, loaf or round
1 cup chopped candied fruit

1. Beat the ricotta and the sugar together thoroughly. Add the chocolate and the almond flavoring and beat again.

2. Slice the cake into 3 or 4 layers. Spread the inside layers with the cheese mixture. Frost the top with any chocolate frosting and decorate it with candied fruit. Chill for several hours before serving.

CHOCOLATE PEPPERMINT ROLL

4 eggs, separated
1 cup granulated sugar
¼ cup water
1 teaspoon vanilla extract
¾ cup sifted flour
6 tablespoons cocoa
¼ teaspoon salt
½ teaspoon cream of tartar
Confectioners' sugar, sifted
2 cups heavy cream
½ cup crushed peppermint-stick candy
Few drops of red food coloring
Blender Fudge Sauce (p. 200)

1. Butter a jelly-roll pan (10 x 15 inches), line it with wax paper, and butter the paper.

2. Beat the egg yolks until they are thick. Add ½ cup of the granulated sugar gradually, then add the water and vanilla. Beat until thick and smooth.

3. Sift the flour, cocoa, and salt together. Fold these gently into the yolk-sugar mixture.

4. Beat the egg whites until they are frothy, and add the cream of tartar. Begin to add the remaining ½ cup of granulated sugar, a little at a time, beating as you add. When it forms soft peaks, fold the meringue carefully into the rest of the mixture. Spread on the prepared pan.

5. Bake in a 325° F. oven until the cake is springy to the touch and shrinks from the sides of the pan. Turn out the cake onto a tea towel sprinkled with confectioners' sugar. Cut off the crisp edges, and starting at the narrow end, roll up the cake with the towel inside. Cool.

6. When cold, unroll, and remove the towel. Whip the cream until stiff; add the candy and food coloring and blend. Spread the cake with the whipped-cream mixture. Roll up again. Dust with more confectioners' sugar. Chill before serving. Slice, and serve with ice cream and hot Blender Fudge Sauce.

Variations: CHOCOLATE RUM ROLL

Spread the cold cake with Rum Custard Filling (p. 99) or Mocha Rum Butter Filling (pp. 100–101). Roll it up again and dust with confectioners' sugar. Place the cake on a serving tray and decorate with sprigs of holly in the winter or fresh mint leaves in the summer.

CHOCOLATE CREAM ROLL

Spread the cold cake with whipped cream flavored with Chokaulu. Roll it up and chill.
To serve: Slice the cake and top with a scoop of coffee ice cream. Pass your favorite chocolate sauce.

GÉNOISE AU CHOCOLAT

A lovely, delicate cake. You may ice it, as directed below, or use it for petits fours.

½ cup unsalted butter
5 ounces dark sweet chocolate
¼ cup water
5 eggs
½ cup plus 1 tablespoon sugar

1 cup minus 2 tablespoons sifted flour
1 tablespoon vanilla extract
Chocolate Pastry Cream (pp. 96–97)
Chocolate Satin Icing (p. 111)

1. Prepare an 8 x 2-inch springform pan by greasing it with unsalted butter and dusting it with cocoa.

2. Melt the butter and set it aside to cool.

3. Melt the chocolate in water in the top of a double boiler, over simmering water. Blend and set aside to cool.

4. Beat the eggs until light and lemon-colored. Add the sugar slowly as you beat, and continue to beat until the mixture ribbons. This may take 10 to 15 minutes. At any rate, do not skimp on the beating.

5. Stir the chocolate into the egg and sugar mixture. Then add the vanilla. Gently fold in the flour, and then add the melted butter, discarding the milky sediment. Pour the batter into the prepared pan.

6. Bake in a 350° F. oven for 45 minutes. Cool. Split and fill with Chocolate Pastry Cream, and ice with Chocolate Satin Icing.

Note: I like to spread a thin layer of seedless raspberry jam on the cake before putting on the Chocolate Pastry Cream.

GOLDEN ANGEL FOOD

This cake is a delight by itself, but spread it with apricot jam, and add chocolate icing, and you have a perfect dessert.

6 eggs, separated
½ cup cold water
1⅓ cups sugar
2 teaspoons vanilla extract
1 teaspoon almond extract
1½ cups sifted flour
Pinch of salt

1 teaspoon cream of tartar
Apricot jam
Glossy Chocolate Frosting
  (p. 118) or Bittersweet
  Chocolate Frosting
  (p. 104)

1. Beat the egg yolks until they are thick and lemon-colored. Add the water and beat well again. Add the sugar gradually, and beat until the mixture is thick and creamy. Mix in the flavorings.

2. Sift the flour and salt together 3 times. Sift the mixture, a little at a time, over the batter, folding it in gently.

3. Whip the egg whites until they are foamy. Add the cream of tartar and continue to beat until they are stiff. Fold these gently into the batter. Pour into an ungreased 10-inch tube pan.

4. Bake in a 350° F. oven for 1 hour. Invert the pan until the cake is cold. Turn it out. Spread it with apricot jam, and frost with Glossy Chocolate Frosting or Bittersweet Chocolate Frosting.

HAZELNUT ROLL

A wonderful rich dessert.

7 eggs, separated
¾ cup granulated sugar
1½ cups hazelnuts, finely
   ground or put through
   an electric blender
1 teaspoon baking powder

2 tablespoons brandy
Confectioners' sugar, sifted
Wine Custard Filling
  (p. 101)
Chocolate Buttercream Ic-
  ing (p. 106)

1. Butter a jelly-roll pan (10 x 15 inches), fit wax paper in the bottom, and butter the wax paper.

2. Beat the egg yolks till they are thick and lemon-colored. Add the granulated sugar, and continue to beat until the mixture is thick and smooth. Beat in the nuts and the baking powder.

3. Whip the egg whites until they are stiff but not dry. Add the brandy and fold the two mixtures together. Spread in the prepared pan.

4. Bake in a 350° F. oven for 15 to 20 minutes, or until the cake is springy to the touch. Turn the cake out on a tea towel dusted with confectioners' sugar. Cut off the crusts on the edges, roll up the cake from the narrow end with the towel inside, and cool.

5. Unroll the cake, remove the towel, spread Wine Custard Filling on it, and roll it up again. Frost with Chocolate Buttercream Icing.

ITALIAN RUM CAKE

If you have ever made that well-known Italian dessert zabaglione, *this recipe will have a familiar ring.*

8 egg yolks	1 cup heavy cream,
1 cup sugar	whipped
½ cup sherry	1 cup chopped candied
1 spongecake, loaf or	fruit
round	Chocolate Curls (p. 126)
1 cup dark rum	

1. Put the egg yolks and sugar in the top of a double boiler over boiling water. At no time should the boiling water touch the bottom of the boiler top. Beat yolks and sugar until thick and light. Add the sherry slowly, beating all the while. The mixture will thicken and double in bulk. Remove from the heat and cool. Fold in the cream and the fruit.

2. Slice the spongecake into 2 or 3 horizontal layers. Pour rum over the lower layers, and then spread the cold custard over them and on the outside of the cake. Decorate the top with Chocolate Curls.

Chill well before serving.

CAKES MADE WITH BUTTERMILK, SOUR MILK, OR CREAM

CHOCOLATE VELVET ALMOND CAKE

Even though this is easy to put together, its texture does not suffer. You'll receive compliments on this cake.

1⅔ cups flour
1½ cups sugar
¾ cup cocoa
1½ teaspoons baking soda
1 teaspoon salt
½ cup soft butter
1½ cups buttermilk

2 eggs
1 tablespoon vanilla extract
1 cup chopped toasted almonds
Chocolate Velvet Frosting (p. 112)

1. Butter a cake pan (13 x 9 x 2 inches) and dust with cocoa.

2. Sift the flour, sugar, cocoa, baking soda, and salt into a mixing bowl. Add the butter, buttermilk, eggs, and vanilla. Blend with the mixer on low speed, then beat at medium speed for 3 minutes. Stir in ⅔ cup of the almonds and pour the batter into the prepared pan.

3. Bake in a 350° F. oven for 30 minutes, or until the cake is springy to the touch and shrinks away from the sides of the pan.

4. Frost with Easy Chocolate Velvet Frosting and sprinkle the rest of the almonds on top.

COCOA PECAN LAYER CAKE

An elegant cake, tender and moist.

½ cup butter
2 cups firmly packed
  brown sugar
2 eggs
2 teaspoons vanilla extract
¼ cup cocoa
⅔ cup water
2¼ cups sifted flour

1 teaspoon baking soda
1 teaspoon salt
⅔ cup sour cream
¾ cup pecans, coarsely
  chopped
Chocolate Whipped Cream
  II (p. 98)
Fudge Frosting
  (pp. 117–118)

1. Butter two 9-inch layer-cake pans and dust them with cocoa.

2. Cream the butter with the sugar until the mixture is light and fluffy. Add the eggs, one at a time, beating after each addition. Add the vanilla. Stir in the cocoa which has been mixed with the water.

3. Sift the flour, baking soda, and salt together. Add to the first mixture alternately with the sour cream. Stir in the nuts. Spread on the prepared pans.

4. Bake in a 350° F. oven for 30 to 35 minutes, or until the cake is springy to the touch and shrinks from the sides of the pans.

5. Put the cake together with Chocolate Whipped Cream II and spread Fudge Frosting on the top.

FUDGE PECAN CAKE

An easy-to-mix cake. If you're really in a hurry, use one of the frosting mixes, but add a little extra vanilla if you do.

2 cups sifted flour
1¼ cups sugar
1½ teaspoons baking pow-
    der
½ teaspoon baking soda
1 teaspoon salt
½ cup soft butter
1 cup buttermilk
1 teaspoon vanilla

3 eggs
4 ounces unsweetened choc-
    olate (squares, melted
    and cooled, or envelopes)
¾ cup coarsely chopped
    pecans
Creamy Chocolate Frosting
    (p. 115)

1. Butter an 8-inch-square cake pan and dust it with cocoa.

2. Sift flour, sugar, baking powder, baking soda, and salt into a mixing bowl. Add butter, buttermilk, vanilla, eggs, and chocolate. Blend on low speed, then turn the mixer up to medium and beat for 3 minutes. Stir in the nuts and spread the batter in prepared pan.

3. Bake in a 350° F. oven for 35 to 40 minutes, or until the cake is springy to the touch and shrinks from the sides of the pan. Cool for 10 minutes, and then turn it out onto a cake rack to cool.

Frost with Creamy Chocolate Frosting.

EGGLESS CHOCOLATE CAKE

This is a simple cake, fine for an occasion when a not-too-rich cake is desired.

½ cup butter
1 cup sugar
2 ounces chocolate
    (squares, melted,
    or envelopes)

2 cups sifted flour
1 teaspoon baking soda
1 cup sour milk
1 teaspoon vanilla extract
Confectioners' sugar, sifted

1. Butter a 9-inch-square pan. Line it with wax paper and butter the paper.

2. Cream the butter and sugar together thoroughly. Stir in the chocolate.

3. Sift the flour and baking soda together and add to the first mixture alternately with the sour milk. Stir in the vanilla. Pour the batter into the prepared pan.

4. Bake in a 350° F. oven for 25 to 30 minutes, or until the cake is springy to the touch and shrinks from the sides of the pan.

5. Turn the cake out onto a cake rack, and remove the paper. When cool, shake confectioners' sugar over the top. Cut into squares.

FAVORITE DEVIL'S FOOD

2 ounces chocolate (envelopes or squares, melted)	2 eggs
½ cup boiling water	2½ cups sifted flour
½ cup butter	1 teaspoon baking powder
2 cups firmly packed brown sugar	1 teaspoon baking soda
	¼ teaspoon salt
	½ cup sour milk
	1 teaspoon vanilla extract
	Mocha Frosting (p. 119)

1. Butter two 9-inch layer-cake pans and dust with cocoa.

2. Stir chocolate and boiling water together until well blended. Cool.

3. Cream the butter and brown sugar until light and fluffy. Add the eggs, one at a time, beating well after each addition. Add the cooled chocolate mixture.

4. Sift the dry ingredients together and add to the first mixture alternately with the sour milk. Stir in the vanilla. Pour into the prepared pans.

5. Bake in a 375° F. oven for 30 to 35 minutes, or until the cake is springy in the center and shrinks from the sides of the pans. Cool.

6. Cut into squares. Ice tops and sides with Mocha Frosting. The tops may be sprinkled with ground nuts.

PARTY CHOCOLATE CAKE

This is a glamorous three-layer cake, a company "special."

6 ounces chocolate (squares, melted, or envelopes)
1½ cups hot water
1 cup butter
3 cups sugar
4 eggs
1 tablespoon vanilla extract
4 cups sifted flour

1½ teaspoons baking soda
1 teaspoon baking powder
1 teaspoon salt
⅔ cup sour milk
Pistachio nuts, finely chopped
Chocolate Whipped Cream I (p. 98)
Chocolate Butter Icing (pp. 106–107)

1. Butter three 8-inch layer-cake pans and dust them with cocoa.

2. Combine the chocolate and water. Stir until blended. Cool.

3. Cream the butter and sugar until light and fluffy. Add the eggs, one at a time, beating after each addition. Stir in the vanilla.

4. Sift the flour, baking soda, baking powder, and salt together. Add to the butter and sugar mixture a little at a time, alternating with the sour milk. Stir in the chocolate mixture. Spread in the prepared pans.

5. Bake in a 375° F. oven for 30 to 35 minutes, or until the cake is springy in the center and shrinks away from the sides of the pans. Cool for 10 minutes in the pans, and then turn out on cake racks to cool.

6. When cold, spread Chocolate Whipped Cream I between the layers, and frost with the Chocolate Butter Icing, saving enough of the icing for the final touch. Press the chopped pistachios on the sides of the cake. Pipe the remaining icing through a pastry tube around the edge, top and bottom, to give it an attractive finish.

RAISIN CHOCOLATE CAKE

A lovely moist cake, deliciously filled with raisins and nuts.

½ cup butter	¾ teaspoon baking soda
1¼ cups sugar	¼ teaspoon salt
1 egg	½ cup seedless raisins
2 ounces chocolate	½ cup English walnuts
(squares, melted, or en-	1½ cups sour cream
velopes)	1 teaspoon vanilla extract
2½ cups flour	Fudge Frosting
2 teaspoons baking powder	(pp. 117–118)

1. Butter 2 layer-cake pans and dust them with cocoa.

2. Cream the butter and the sugar until they are light and fluffy. Add the egg and beat well. Stir in the cooled chocolate.

3. Sift the dry ingredients together. Shake a little over the raisins and nuts.

4. Beat the dry ingredients into the butter mixture alternately with the sour cream. Add the vanilla. Stir in the nuts and raisins. Pour the batter into the prepared pans.

5. Bake in a 375° F. oven for 30 to 35 minutes, or until the cake is springy to the touch and shrinks away from the sides of the pans. Cool for 10 minutes. Turn out on cake racks.

6. When cold, frost with Fudge Frosting.

SOUR-CREAM CHOCOLATE CAKE

Thrifty and not too rich, this is an everyday favorite.

3 ounces chocolate
(squares, melted, or en-
velopes)
½ cup hot water
1½ cups sugar
1 cup sour cream

1 tablespoon vanilla ex-
tract
2 eggs
2 cups sifted flour
1½ teaspoons baking soda
½ teaspoon salt
Fluffy Cocoa Frosting
(p. 116)

1. Butter a cake pan (13 x 9 x 2 inches) and dust it with cocoa.

2. Combine the chocolate and hot water. Blend thoroughly and set aside to cool.

3. Beat sugar, sour cream, and vanilla together. Add the eggs, one at a time, beating after each addition. Add cooled chocolate mixture.

4. Sift flour, baking soda, and salt together. Add to the first mixture in small amounts while you beat. Pour into prepared pan.

5. Bake in a 350° F. oven for 35 to 40 minutes, or until the cake is springy to the touch and shrinks away from the sides of the pan.

6. Fluffy Cocoa Frosting is perfect on this cake.

CAKES MADE WITH YEAST

FEATHERLIGHT CHOCOLATE LOAF CAKE

This is a cake made with yeast, using the "cool-rise" principle recommended for making bread. You put the cake together, place it in the refrigerator overnight, and bake it the following day.

First Day

1 envelope dry yeast	3 ounces chocolate
¼ cup warm water	(squares, melted, or en-
½ cup butter	velopes)
1⅓ cups sugar	2 cups sifted flour
2 eggs	1 teaspoon salt
	⅔ cup milk

1. Dissolve the yeast in the warm water.

2. Cream the butter and sugar together until light and fluffy. Add the eggs, one at a time, beating after each addition. Stir in the cooled chocolate and the yeast and mix well.

3. Sift the flour and salt together and add to the creamed mixture alternately with the milk. Cover the bowl and place in the refrigerator.

Second Day

¾ teaspoon baking soda	1½ teaspoons vanilla ex-
2 tablespoons warm water	tract

1. Butter a loaf pan (about 8 x 4 x 3 inches).

2. Mix the baking soda and water. Stir into the batter. Add the vanilla. Mix well and pour into the prepared pan.

3. Bake in a 350° F. oven for 35 to 40 minutes, or until the cake shrinks from the sides of the pan and a wooden pick comes out clean when inserted in the center. Remove from pan and cool.

SOURDOUGH CHOCOLATE CAKE

If you are a sourdough enthusiast, you will want to try this cake. For it, you have to have a "starter," which is reminiscent of grandmother's recipe for buckwheat pancakes. You will find the cake hearty, but not too rich, and not really "sour."

Starter

1 envelope dry yeast	2 cups flour
1 cup warm water	1 cup cool water

1. In a large mixing bowl, not a metal one, dissolve the yeast in the water and beat in 1 cup of the flour. Cover the bowl and let it stand in a warm place for 48 hours, or until the mixture ferments.

2. Stir in another cup of flour and the cool water, mix well, and let the mixture stand overnight. The next morning, the starter is ready to use. Take out what you need and store the rest in the refrigerator for future use.

Cake

6 tablespoons butter	½ teaspoon salt
1 cup sugar	½ cup starter
1 egg	2 ounces chocolate
1 teaspoon vanilla extract	(squares, melted, or en-
1½ cups sifted flour	velopes)
1 teaspoon baking soda	½ cup hot water

1. Butter a baking pan (13 x 9 x 2 inches).

2. Cream the butter and sugar together until light and fluffy. Beat in the egg and vanilla.

3. Sift the flour, baking soda, and salt together, and add to the first mixture alternately with the starter. Blend the chocolate with the hot water and cool it; then stir the mixture into the batter and beat until all is well blended. Pour the batter into the prepared pan.

4. Bake in a 350° F. oven for 35 to 40 minutes, or until the cake shrinks from the sides of the pan and a wooden pick inserted in the center comes out clean.

BRAZIL-NUT CHIFFON CAKE

A delightfully different cake.

1 cup plus 2 tablespoons sifted flour
¾ cup sugar
1½ teaspoons baking powder
½ teaspoon salt
¼ cup salad oil

4 eggs, separated
¼ cup cold water
1 teaspoon vanilla extract
¼ teaspoon cream of tartar
1 cup chopped Brazil nuts
Glossy Chocolate Frosting (p. 118)

1. Sift flour, sugar, baking powder, and salt into a mixing bowl. Add the oil, egg yolks, water, and vanilla. Beat at low speed to blend.

2. Beat egg whites until frothy throughout, add cream of tartar, and beat until very stiff. Fold into the first mixture. Fold in the chopped nuts. Pour into an ungreased 10-inch tube pan.

3. Bake in a 325° F. oven for 50 to 55 minutes, or until cake is springy to the touch. Invert to cool.

4. Remove from the pan and frost with Glossy Chocolate Frosting.

BROWN VELVET PARTY CAKE

Incredibly light, deliciously dark.

8 eggs, separated
½ teaspoon cream of tartar
1¾ cups sugar
2¼ cups sifted flour
3 teaspoons baking powder
1 teaspoon salt
½ cup salad oil
¾ cup water

1 tablespoon vanilla extract
4 ounces unsweetened chocolate (squares, melted and cooled, or envelopes)
Chocolate Butter Icing (pp. 106–107)

1. Whip the egg whites with the cream of tartar until they stand in soft peaks. Beat in ¾ cup of the sugar, slowly, until all is used. Beat until a very stiff meringue is formed.

2. Sift flour, remaining 1 cup sugar, the baking powder, and salt into the large bowl of an electric mixer. Slowly pour in the oil, water, and vanilla. When blended, add the egg yolks, two at a time, beating after each addition. Then mix in the cooled chocolate.

3. Fold in the meringue. Spoon into a 10-inch tube cake pan. Cut through batter with a spatula to remove air holes.

4. Bake in a 325° F. oven for about 1¼ hours, or until the cake is springy to the touch.

5. Invert the pan to cool the cake before taking it out of the pan. Slice horizontally into three layers.

Fill and frost with Chocolate Butter Icing; you will need to make 2½ times the recipe.

HONEY COCOA CAKE

This cake contains so many luscious ingredients, it is completely irresistible.

2 eggs	Pinch of salt
⅔ cup sugar	¾ teaspoon baking powder
½ cup cocoa	½ teaspoon baking soda
½ cup hot water	1 cup almonds, chopped
½ cup honey	2 tablespoons cognac
1 tablespoon salad oil	Coffee Syrup (p. 206)
1¾ cups sifted flour	Whipped cream

1. Butter a 9-inch-square pan, line it with wax paper, and butter the paper.

2. Beat the eggs until they are thick and creamy. Beat in the sugar.

3. Mix the cocoa, hot water, honey, and salad oil. Blend. Beat this into the egg mixture.

4. Sift the flour, salt, baking powder, and baking soda together and add to the batter, a little at a time. Stir the nuts in. Add the cognac. Pour into the prepared pan.

5. Bake in a 325° F. oven for 45 minutes.

6. Meanwhile make Coffee Syrup. Pour the syrup over the cake when it comes out of the oven. Cool.
To serve, spread whipped cream on top and cut into squares.

MARBLE CHIFFON CAKE

For that unlikely occasion when you can't decide between a white cake and a chocolate one, this marble chiffon presents the perfect answer.

3 ounces chocolate (squares, melted, or envelopes)
3 tablespoons sugar
¼ cup boiling water
3½ teaspoons vanilla extract
2¼ cups sifted flour
1½ cups sugar

3 teaspoons baking powder
1 teaspoon salt
½ cup salad oil (not olive)
7 eggs, separated
¾ cup cold water
1 tablespoon vanilla extract
½ teaspoon cream of tartar
Bittersweet Chocolate Frosting (p. 104)

1. Blend the first four ingredients and set aside.

2. Sift flour, 1½ cups sugar, baking powder, and salt into the bowl of your mixer. Make a well in the center. Pour in the oil, egg yolks, cold water, and 1 tablespoon vanilla and set aside. Beat on low speed to blend, then on medium speed until batter is smooth and creamy.

3. Whip egg whites and cream of tartar until stiff. Pour the batter slowly over them, folding as you pour.

4. Take out one third of the batter and fold the chocolate mixture into it.

5. Pour half of the remaining batter into an ungreased 10-inch angel-food pan. Top with half of the chocolate mixture. Repeat.

With a spatula, cut through the batters, using a circular motion to mix slightly.

6. Bake in a 325° F. oven for 55 minutes, then increase heat to 350° F. for 10 minutes more, or until cake is springy in the center. Invert pan to cool.

7. Remove the cake to a rack and frost with Bittersweet Chocolate Frosting.

REGAL CHOCOLATE LAYER CAKE

5 ounces chocolate (squares, melted, or envelopes)	1¼ cups water
	1 tablespoon vanilla extract
1¾ cups sifted flour	3 eggs
1¼ teaspoons baking soda	Grated semisweet chocolate
¼ teaspoon baking powder	Walnut Filling (p. 101) or
1 teaspoon salt	Chocolate Filling for
1¾ cups sugar	Torten (p. 96)
⅔ cup soft butter	Chantilly Cream (p. 95)

1. Butter four 8-inch layer-cake pans and dust them with cocoa.

2. Put the dry ingredients, the butter, water, chocolate, and vanilla in the bowl of a mixer. Turn on at low speed to blend. Mix at medium speed for 2 minutes. Add the eggs and beat for 2 minutes more. Pour into the prepared pans.

3. Bake in a 350° F. oven for 15 minutes, or until the layers are springy to the touch and shrink from the sides of the pan. Place on a cake rack for 10 minutes, then turn out to cool completely. Spread first and third layers with Walnut Filling or Chocolate Filling for Torten.

Spread second layer and top with Chantilly Cream.

Sprinkle the grated semisweet chocolate around the edge.

TORTEN

*T*HIS SECTION contains recipes for the fabulous *Torten,* conceived by Austrian pastry cooks of days gone by. These are the classic recipes which one cannot improve, nor should one try. Rich, yet delicate, and indescribably delicious, they intrigue the aspiring cook who does not regard the cake mix as the ultimate in culinary art.

Technically speaking, a *Torte* uses no shortening, baking powder, or flour. Bread crumbs and ground nuts take the place of the latter, and the cake is leavened with eggs. The resulting cake is flat, rather than light and fluffy.

From the aesthetic point of view, *Torten* should be partaken of to the strains of a Strauss waltz.

ALMOND CHOCOLATE TORTE

A recipe from Vienna, that city of unexcelled cooks.

5 eggs, separated
¾ cup (12 tablespoons) sugar
1 extra egg yolk
2 ounces chocolate (squares, melted, or envelopes)

1 teaspoon almond extract
1 cup sifted flour
Almond Pastry Cream (p. 95) or Creamy Chocolate Frosting (p. 115)
Whipped cream
Chopped toasted almonds

1. Beat egg whites until foamy. Add 6 tablespoons of the sugar gradually, beating as you add.

2. In a separate bowl beat the 6 egg yolks until thick, and add the rest of the sugar, beating until thick and creamy. Add the cooled chocolate and the almond extract to the yolk mixture and fold in. Then fold in the egg whites. Sift a little flour at a time over the mixture and fold in, repeating until all of the flour is used. Pour into an ungreased 10-inch tube pan.

3. Bake in a 350° F. oven for 45 minutes. Invert the pan until the cake is cold.

4. Remove the *Torte* from the pan and slice into 3 layers. Spread two of the layers with Almond Pastry Cream or Creamy Chocolate Frosting and put the layers together. Spread whipped cream on the top layer. Sprinkle with chopped toasted almonds.

Makes 8–10 servings.

ALMOND RICE TORTE

An unusual layered custardlike dessert of intriguing flavor.

Crust

½ cup butter
¼ cup sugar
2 egg yolks
1 teaspoon almond extract

1½ cups sifted flour
1 teaspoon baking powder
¼ teaspoon salt
1 cup toasted almonds

1. Cream the butter with the sugar until light and creamy. Beat in the egg yolks, one at a time, beating after each addition. Stir in the flavoring.

2. Sift the flour, baking powder, and salt together and add to the batter. This makes a very stiff dough that may have to be kneaded by hand to incorporate all of the flour. Press the dough into an ungreased 10-inch springform pan, covering the bottom, and about halfway up the sides. Sprinkle the almonds on top of this crust.

Filling

3 cups milk	¾ cup sugar
3 ounces chocolate	Pinch of salt
(squares, cut up, or en-	3 egg yolks
velopes)	1 teaspoon almond extract
⅔ cup uncooked rice	

1. Place the milk, chocolate, rice, sugar, and salt in the top of a double boiler. Cook over boiling water, stirring occasionally, until the rice is done. This will take from 45 to 60 minutes.

2. Beat the egg yolks well. Stir in a little of the hot mixture, then return all to the double boiler. Stir for a minute or two, then remove from the heat. Cool slightly and add the almond extract. Pour into the crust-lined pan on top of the almonds.

Topping

1 egg	1 tablespoon dark rum
1 cup heavy cream	

1. Beat the egg; add cream and rum. Pour gently over the filling. Bake the *Torte* in a 350° F. oven for 45 minutes. Remove to a rack to cool.

2. When the *Torte* is cold, remove the springform pan and transfer cake to a serving plate.

To Serve: Cut the cake into wedges, and top with whipped cream.

Makes 8 servings.

CHOCOLATE HAZELNUT TORTE

8 eggs, separated
4 extra egg yolks
1 cup sugar
¼ pound hazelnuts
¼ pound walnuts
¼ cup chocolate bits
Pinch of salt

1 tablespoon fine bread
crumbs
Whipped cream
Crème de cacao
Chocolate Frosting for
Torten (p. 108)

1. Beat the 12 egg yolks. Add the sugar and beat until thick and creamy.

2. Put the nut meats and the chocolate bits through an electric blender and stir them into the egg-yolk mixture.

3. Beat the egg whites with the salt until stiff. Fold them into the batter. Then fold in the crumbs. Spread the batter in a buttered 10-inch springform pan.

4. Bake in a 350° F. oven for 40 minutes. Cool.

5. Split into 2 layers. Fill with whipped cream flavored with crème de cacao, poured with a generous hand. Spread Chocolate Frosting for Torten on top.

Makes 6–8 servings.

CHOCOLATE WALNUT MERINGUE

3 egg whites
¾ cup sugar
1 teaspoon vanilla extract
Few grains of salt
½ cup walnuts

2 cups chocolate-wafer
crumbs
1 teaspoon baking powder
Coffee ice cream
Blender Fudge Sauce
(p. 200)

1. Butter a 9-inch glass pie pan.

2. Beat the egg whites until they are stiff, and add the sugar gradually while you continue to beat. Add the vanilla and the salt.

3. Grind the nuts fine, or put them through an electric blender.

Mix them with the chocolate-wafer crumbs and add the baking powder. Fold this gently into the egg whites. Spread on the prepared dish.

4. Bake in a 325° F. oven for 40 minutes. Cool.

5. To serve, cut into wedges or squares, top with coffee ice cream, and pass Hot Fudge Sauce.

Makes 6 servings.

CONTINENTAL TORTE

We like this especially made with hazelnuts, but any nuts may be used.

Torte

4 egg whites	½ cup hazelnuts,
1½ cups sugar	put through a blender or finely ground.

1. Line four 8-inch layer-cake pans with unglazed paper.

2. Beat the egg whites until stiff, but not dry. Add the sugar very slowly, beating as you add. Beat in the nuts, except for 2 tablespoons of them which are saved for the top. Spread the meringue in thin layers in the prepared pans.

3. Bake in a 250° F. oven for 20–30 minutes. Turn off the heat, and leave the meringues in the oven with the door slightly open for 15 minutes. Turn out, remove paper, and cool on cake racks.

Filling

2 egg whites	1 cup soft butter
½ cup sugar	Seedless raspberry jam
4 tablespoons cocoa	Confectioners' sugar, sifted

1. Beat the egg whites in the top of a double boiler until foamy throughout. Beat in the sugar and cocoa, mixed. Add the soft butter and continue beating until of proper consistency to spread. Cool.

2. Put the layers together with a thin layer of jam topped with the filling. Shake confectioners' sugar over the top of the cake, and sprinkle the remaining nuts on this.

DOBOSCHTORTE

The secret of success with this Torte *lies in the thinness of the layers.*

5 eggs, separated
½ cup sugar
1 tablespoon lemon juice
½ cup sifted flour

¼ teaspoon salt
Chocolate Buttercream Icing (p. 106)

1. Prepare three 9-inch layer-cake pans having removable bottoms. Butter them and dust with flour.

2. Beat the egg yolks until thick and lemon-colored. Beat in the sugar and then the lemon juice, and continue beating until the mixture is thick and creamy.

3. Sift the flour and salt into a bowl. Stir the egg mixture into this.

4. Beat the egg whites until stiff. Fold these gently into the batter. Spread 4 or 5 tablespoons of the batter on each pan.

5. Bake the layers in a 350° F. oven for 5 minutes, or until delicately browned. Turn out onto a cake rack. Repeat this until all the batter is used. You should have 8 to 10 layers. Cool.

6. Put the cake together with Chocolate Buttercream Icing. Chill overnight before serving.

FAIR LADY TORTE

This is a quick way to a divine dessert—you buy the cake.

1 spongecake loaf
1 recipe Chocolate Pastry Cream II (p. 97)
2 cups heavy cream
2 tablespoons confectioners' sugar
1 teaspoon unflavored gelatin
1 teaspoon vanilla extract
Pistachio nuts, ground
Chocolate Curls (p. 126)

1. Slice the spongecake into 3 horizontal layers. Spread the 2 bottom layers with the Chocolate Pastry Cream II.

2. Whip the cream with the sugar and the gelatin. Add the vanilla. Spread on the outside of the loaf. Cover the top with the nuts and Chocolate Curls.

MERINGUE LAYER CAKE OR TORTE

An unusual light, delicious dessert. This freezes well, so you can make 2 cakes, and have one for later.

Cake

4 egg whites
1½ cups granulated sugar
⅓ cup finely ground almonds
Confectioners' sugar, sifted
Chocolate Curls (p. 126)

1. Butter 4 layer-cake pans with removable bottoms. Cover each pan with a round of unglazed paper.

2. Beat the egg whites until stiff, and gradually add in the granulated sugar and the almonds. Spread the meringue on the 4 pans.

3. Bake in a 250° F. oven for 25 minutes. Turn the meringues over and bake for another 5 minutes. Remove the paper and cool.

Filling

2 egg whites	4 ounces (squares) semisweet chocolate, melted
½ cup sugar	
2 tablespoons cocoa	1 tablespoon vanilla extract
1 cup soft unsalted butter	

1. Put the egg whites in the top of a double boiler over simmering water and beat until foamy. Gradually beat in the sugar, and cocoa, butter, and chocolate. Beat well. Cool.

2. Spread the filling between the meringue layers. Dust confectioners' sugar on top. Decorate with Chocolate Curls. Chill for 24 hours before serving.

Variation: MOCHA MERINGUE LAYERS

Make the meringue layers using these ingredients:

6 egg whites	1 teaspoon instant coffee powder
1½ cups sugar	

Bake as directed above, and fill with Mocha Pastry Cream Filling (p. 100).

MOCHA TORTE

This is one of the best of all the chocolate Torten.

Cake

4 ounces semisweet chocolate	4 eggs
¼ cup water	½ cup sugar
1 teaspoon instant coffee powder	1 teaspoon vanilla extract
	½ cup unsifted flour
¼ teaspoon salt	¾ cup walnut meats, ground very fine or put through your blender

1. Butter a 9-inch cake pan, such as a layer-cake pan. Line the bottom with wax paper and butter that too.

2. Place the chocolate, water, coffee powder, and salt in a saucepan and stir over low heat until the chocolate is melted and the whole blended. Set aside to cool.

3. Beat the eggs well and add the sugar slowly, beating until the mixture is thick and creamy. Add the cooled chocolate and the vanilla.

4. Sift the flour three times and fold gently into the batter. Fold in half of the nuts. Pour into the prepared pan.

5. Bake in a 350° F. oven for 30 minutes, or until the cake is springy to the touch and shrinks from the side of the pan. Turn out on a cake rack and remove the wax paper. Cool.

Glaze

3 ounces semisweet chocolate	¼ cup corn syrup
	1 tablespoon water

1. Simmer all together over low heat until smooth.

2. Pour the glaze over the cold *Torte* and sprinkle the rest of the walnuts on top.

NORWEGIAN NUT TORTE

A delicious Torte *with an authentic foreign air.*

¼ cup fine bread crumbs	1 teaspoon grated lemon rind
1½ cups finely ground filberts or hazelnuts	Cinnamon Icing (p. 112) or Chocolate Frosting for Torten (p. 108)
¾ cup sugar	
½ cup cocoa	
4 eggs, separated	
1 tablespoon vanilla extract	

1. Butter a baking pan (8 x 8 x 2 inches) and dust with the bread crumbs.

2. Mix the nuts, sugar, and cocoa in a mixing bowl. Beat in the egg yolks, vanilla, and lemon rind.

3. Beat the egg whites until they are stiff but not dry, and gently fold them into the first mixture. Spread in the prepared pan.

4. Bake in a 350° F. oven for 30 minutes.

5. Chill before serving. Cinnamon Icing is good on this, or try Chocolate Frosting for Torten.

NUT LAYER SPONGE

This is much like a Torte. *The elderberry jam gives it a flavor all its own.*

¼ cup butter	2 teaspoons cream of tar-
⅓ cup confectioners' sugar	tar
5 eggs, separated	½ cup ground walnuts
⅓ cup sifted flour	Seedless elderberry jam
1 teaspoon baking powder	Creamy Chocolate Frosting
Pinch of salt	(p. 115)

1. Butter two 9-inch layer-cake pans and dust them with flour.

2. Cream the butter and sugar until light and fluffy. Add the egg yolks, one at a time, beating after each addition.

3. Sift flour, baking powder, and salt.

4. Beat the egg whites until frothy throughout. Add the cream of tartar and continue to beat until stiff but not dry. Fold them into the batter alternately with the dry ingredients. Fold in the nuts. Spread in the prepared pan.

5. Bake in a 350° F. oven for 20 minutes. Cool and turn out onto cake racks. When cold, spread the layers with the jam, and frost the top and sides with Creamy Chocolate Frosting.

SACHERTORTE

Everyone who is a connoisseur of good food has heard of the legendary hostelry, the Hotel Sacher, where this Torte was created. There is nothing more delectable than this traditional cake.

¾ cup butter	6 ounces chocolate
¾ cup sugar	(squares, melted, or en-
6 eggs, separated	velopes)
1 teaspoon vanilla extract	1¾ cups sifted flour
	Apricot jam

1. Butter 2 layer-cake pans and dust them with flour.

2. Cream the butter and sugar, beating until thick and creamy. Add the egg yolks, one at a time, and beat after each addition. Add the vanilla and the chocolate, melted and cooled.

3. Sift the flour over the batter, a little at a time, and fold in gently. Beat the egg whites until stiff, and fold in also. Pour into the prepared pans.

4. Bake in a 300° F. oven for 35 minutes. Turn out. Spread with warm apricot jam. When set, cover with the chocolate frosting you like best.

SCHAUMTORTE

Traditionally, this Torte is served with fresh fruit between the layers and whipped cream on top. We like it this way.

6 egg whites	Mocha Pastry Cream
Pinch of salt	(p. 100)
½ teaspoon cream of tartar	1 cup heavy cream
2 cups sugar	1 teaspoon vanilla extract
1½ teaspoons vinegar	Chocolate Curls (p. 126)

1. Fit unglazed white paper in the bottom of two 9-inch layer-cake pans with removable bottoms.

2. Whip the egg whites until quite frothy, then add the salt and cream of tartar. Continue beating until stiff. Then add the sugar, ¼ cup at a time, and the vinegar. Beat until stiff peaks are formed. Spread in the prepared pans.

3. Bake in a 325° F. oven for 45 minutes. Allow the layers to cool in the oven.

4. Turn out, and remove the paper. Fill with Mocha Pastry Cream or with any chocolate filling. Whip the cream, add the vanilla, and spread on top. Arrange the Chocolate Curls around the edge in a wreath.

VIENNESE ALMOND TORTE

A classic Torte.

6 eggs, separated	½ cup dry bread crumbs
1 cup sugar	½ teaspoon almond extract
1 lemon, juice and rind	¼ teaspoon salt
1 teaspoon ground cinnamon	Lemon Glaze (p. 119) or
1 cup unblanched almonds, ground	Rose Icing (p. 121)

1. Beat the egg yolks until thick and lemon-colored. Add the sugar slowly while continuing to beat. When smooth and creamy, add the lemon juice and rind, cinnamon, almonds, crumbs, and almond extract.

2. Whip the egg whites with the salt until stiff but not dry. Fold these into the batter. Pour into a buttered 8-inch tube pan or springform pan.

3. Bake in a 350° F. oven for 40 minutes.

4. While the cake is baking, make the sherry syrup.

Sherry Syrup

¾ cup sherry
2 cloves
1 cinnamon stick
(2 inches)

4 tablespoons sugar
2 tablespoons water

Bring all the syrup ingredients to a boil. Strain. Pour over the cake when it comes out of the oven.

Cool the cake in the pan.

When cold, turn out and spread with Lemon Glaze or Rose Icing.

CAKE FILLINGS, FROSTINGS, AND ICINGS

CAKE FILLINGS

WHEN IT COMES to selecting a filling for a cake, cream puffs, or a *Torte*, there is a delicious variety to choose from. You may like a filling made with chocolate, or prefer to use cocoa. Either way, you will want to have that good chocolatey taste.

There are some fillings sweetened with brown sugar, some with white, while some add honey for that intriguing sweetness that brings forth the full chocolate flavor. You may use egg yolks for richness, or make your filling without them. Some are made with milk or evaporated milk, some are combined with cream, plain or whipped.

The flavoring may be vanilla, coffee, rum, almond, peppermint, orange peel, brandy, or any flavoring or liqueur that appeals to your fancy. They are all delectable, and all blend well with chocolate.

ALMOND PASTRY CREAM

Try this as a filling for your favorite chocolate layer cake.

1 cup blanched almonds
½ cup confectioners' sugar
3 tablespoons butter

1 tablespoon kirsch
2 egg yolks

1. Put the almonds through an electric blender or grind very fine. Add the sugar and mix.

2. Cream the butter; add the kirsch, then the egg yolks, one at a time, beating after each addition. Add the almond-sugar mixture and beat again.

Makes enough to fill a 2-layer cake.

CHANTILLY CREAM (CRÈME CHANTILLY)

1 cup heavy cream
Few grains of salt

2 tablespoons of crème de cacao

Whip the cream, add the salt and the liqueur.

Use this as a cake filling, or serve on any chocolate dessert.

Note: 1 teaspoon of unflavored gelatin added to the cream while it is being whipped, will help it to stand up longer.

CHOCOLATE CUSTARD FILLING

Use this either for cakes or cream puffs.

½ cup sugar
⅓ cup flour
¼ teaspoon salt
2 cups hot rich milk or light cream

2 ounces chocolate
(squares cut up or envelopes)
3 eggs
2 teaspoons vanilla extract
1 tablespoon sherry or rum (optional)

1. Mix the sugar, flour, and salt in the top of a double boiler. Stir in the milk or cream. Add the chocolate and stir directly over low heat until well blended. Cook until thick and smooth.

2. Beat the eggs and pour the hot mixture slowly over them, beating as you add. Return to double boiler top.

3. Place over hot water, and cook until the custard thickens. Cool.

4. Add vanilla and sherry or rum if desired.

CHOCOLATE FILLING FOR TORTEN

6 ounces (squares) semi-sweet chocolate	Pinch of salt
¾ cup butter	2 egg yolks
1¼ cup confectioners' sugar	1 tablespoon rum

1. Melt the chocolate over hot water. Cool.

2. Cream the butter and sugar till fluffy. Add the salt and egg yolks. Beat well, add the rum, and fold in the chocolate. If the filling is too soft, put it in the refrigerator to stiffen a little.

Makes about 2 cups.

CHOCOLATE PASTRY CREAM I

3 ounces chocolate (squares, melted, or envelopes)	4 egg yolks
	4 tablespoons flour
1½ cups milk	½ cup sugar
	1 teaspoon vanilla extract

1. Heat chocolate and milk over low heat until well blended.

2. Beat the egg yolks until thick and lemon-colored. Beat in the flour and sugar, mixed. Slowly stir in the hot chocolate mixture.

Cook and stir over low heat until the mixture comes to a boil. Cool. Add the vanilla.

Makes about 2½ cups.

Variation: PEPPERMINT CHOCOLATE PASTRY CREAM

Omit the vanilla and add ½ cup crushed peppermint stick candy.

CHOCOLATE PASTRY CREAM II

A rich, delicious filling for cakes, Torten, *and cream puffs.*

6 eggs	¼ cup water
1 cup sugar	1 cup soft butter
5 ounces chocolate (squares, melted, or envelopes)	

1. Beat the eggs thoroughly and blend in the sugar. Beat over hot water until thick and smooth. Remove from the heat.

2. Mix the chocolate with the water and stir into the egg mixture. Beat well. While beating, add the butter, bit by bit. Chill.

Makes about 3 cups.

CHOCOLATE RUM BUTTERCREAM

Use this as a frosting, a filling, or both. This can be made quickly in an electric blender.

1 cup semisweet chocolate bits, melted	2 tablespoons confectioners' sugar
¼ cup boiling water	4 egg yolks
1 teaspoon instant coffee powder	½ cup soft butter
	3 tablespoons dark rum

Blend the chocolate, water, coffee powder, and sugar. Cool slightly. Beat in the egg yolks, one at a time, and then the soft butter. Add the rum and beat until smooth.

Makes about 2 cups—enough to spread between 3 8-inch layers or cover the tops and sides of 2 8-inch layers.

CHOCOLATE WHIPPED CREAM I

An easy delicious filling for layer cakes. You may use it as a frosting for an angel-food or chiffon cake.

1½ cups heavy cream
1 teaspoon unflavored gelatin
2 ounces chocolate
(squares, melted and
cooled, or envelopes)

Pinch of salt
1 teaspoon vanilla extract

Whip the cream with the gelatin until stiff. Fold in the chocolate, salt, and vanilla. Spread on cake and serve at once.

Makes about 2½ cups.

CHOCOLATE WHIPPED CREAM II

4 ounces semisweet choco-
late
2 tablespoons corn syrup
2 tablespoons water

1 cup heavy cream,
whipped
1 tablespoon rum

Melt the chocolate with the corn syrup and water. Blend and cool. Fold into the whipped cream, then add the rum.

Makes about 1½ cups.

CUSTARD CREAM FILLING

½ cup sugar
⅓ cup flour
Pinch of salt
2 cups light cream
4 egg yolks, beaten

2 tablespoons butter
1 tablespoon vanilla extract or 2 tablespoons dark rum

1. Mix the sugar, flour, and salt. Scald the cream and stir into the first mixture. Pour the whole mixture slowly over the beaten egg yolks, beating as you pour.

2. Cook this in the top of a double boiler over simmering water until the custard is thick and smooth. Add the butter and stir to blend. Cool and add the flavoring.

Makes about 3 cups or enough to fill 8 large cream puffs.

Variation: RUM CUSTARD FILLING
Add 2 tablespoons of dark rum to the above.

DUTCH CHOCOLATE FILLING

This recipe comes from Holland, as you might guess from the Dutch cocoa called for in the ingredients.

¼ cup sugar
3 tablespoons Dutch cocoa
1 tablespoon cornstarch
1 cup milk

1 tablespoon vanilla extract
1 cup heavy cream, whipped

1. Mix the sugar, cocoa, and cornstarch in the top of a double boiler. Stir in the milk. Cook over boiling water, stirring until the mixture is thick and smooth. Cool. Add the vanilla.

2. Spoon half of the cocoa mixture over the bottom layer of the cake. Fold the rest into the whipped cream, and spread this on top. (For a perfect finish, sprinkle shaved sweet chocolate on top of the cream.)

Makes about 2½ cups, or enough to fill and top two 8-inch layers.

MOCHA PASTRY CREAM FILLING

2 ounces chocolate (squares, melted, or envelopes)
1 cup cream
1 cup extra-strong coffee
5 egg yolks

¾ cup sugar
Pinch of salt
2 teaspoons cornstarch
2 tablespoons milk
1 teaspoon rum

1. Blend the chocolate, cream, and coffee.

2. Beat the egg yolks until light, add the sugar slowly, then the salt. Beat this until it is thick and creamy. Add the chocolate mixture and blend.

3. Mix the cornstarch and milk and stir into the custard mixture. Turn the whole into the top of a double boiler and cook over simmering water until thick and smooth. Cool. Add the rum.

Makes about 3 cups. This will cover 2 layers of a 3-layer cake or fill 8 large cream puffs.

MOCHA RUM BUTTER FILLING

½ cup confectioners' sugar
3 tablespoons cocoa
¾ cup unsalted butter
3 tablespoons dark rum

1 teaspoon instant coffee powder
1 egg yolk

1. Mix the sugar and the cocoa.

2. Cream the butter and add the sugar-cocoa mixture. Add the rum, the coffee powder, and the egg yolk. Mix well to blend.

Spread between layers of a cold cake. Spread the sides and top with your favorite chocolate frosting.

This makes about 1½ cups and will cover a 9-inch layer.

WALNUT FILLING

2 cups walnut meats
½ cup seedless raisins

2 ounces chocolate
(squares, melted, or envelopes)
⅔ cup honey

1. Chop the nuts and raisins coarsely.

2. Stir the chocolate and honey together to blend. Combine the two mixtures. Spread on a cold cake, or a chocolate roll.

Makes about 2¼ cups.

WINE CUSTARD FILLING

½ cup sugar
⅓ cup flour
Pinch of salt

2 cups light cream
5 egg yolks
4 tablespoons sherry
⅛ teaspoon nutmeg

1. Put the sugar, flour, salt, and cream in a saucepan and stir over low heat until the mixture is thick and smooth.

2. Pour this slowly over the egg yolks, beating as you pour. Bring the mixture to the boiling point, but do not allow to boil. Cool. Stir in the sherry and the nutmeg. Spread when cold.

Makes enough to spread between 3 8- or 9-inch layers. Try it with Ginger Chocolate Cake (pp. 45–46).

FROSTINGS AND ICINGS

You will find that these terms are used interchangeably, although *frosting* usually refers to a cooked icing such as Black and White Peppermint Frosting, and *icing* usually means one made with confectioners' or XXXX sugar (such as Mocha Icing), that is not cooked.

In the case of the latter, I always stir an icing over low heat for a few minutes to eliminate the raw sugar taste. This also makes the icing easier to spread smoothly.

Either kind is spread on a cold cake.

Frosting Tips

1. Brush any loose crumbs from the cake with a pastry brush. Place one layer on a plate, upside down. If you lay a piece of wax paper on the plate first, to be eased out later, it keeps the plate clean. With a metal spatula, spread filling or frosting to the edges.

2. Place a second layer over this, top side up, so that the bottoms of the cake will be together. If there is a third layer, place it top side up on this after the frosting or filling is spread on the second one.

3. Frost the sides of the cake first, using plenty of frosting so that you never touch the cake with a bare spatula.

4. Frost the top last.

FROSTINGS	BUTTER	FLUFFY
To frost two 8-inch layers,	you will need 2¼ cups of butter frosting	3¾ cups of fluffy frosting
two 9-inch layers,	you will need 2⅔ cups of butter frosting	4¼ cups of fluffy frosting
one 8-inch square cake,	you will need 1⅓ cups of butter frosting	3 cups of fluffy frosting

FROSTINGS	BUTTER	FLUFFY
one 9-inch square cake,	you will need 2 cups of butter frosting	3⅔ cups of fluffy frosting
9- or 10-inch tube cake,	you will need 2½ to 3 cups of butter frosting	3½ cups of fluffy frosting
2 dozen cupcakes,	you will need 2¼ cups of butter frosting	5½ cups of fluffy frosting

ALMOND PASTE ICING OR FILLING

1 egg white
1 can (8 ounces) almond
  paste

1. As the almond paste is usually too stiff to spread, beat the egg white slightly, and work enough into the almond paste to give it a spreading consistency.

2. Use this between layers, or on top of a cake, spreading Glossy Chocolate Frosting (p. 118) or any other frosting on top of that. Decorate with almond halves arranged in an attractive design.

Makes enough to cover one 8-inch layer.

AMBER FROSTING

This is an interesting frosting, in that it uses molasses.

2 egg whites
¼ cup water
1 cup sugar

2 tablespoons molasses
Pinch of salt
½ teaspoon vanilla extract

Put egg whites, water, sugar, molasses, and salt in the top of a double boiler. Beat with an electric beater over water at medium heat until the mixture is stiff and will stand up in peaks. Remove from the heat and add the vanilla. Spread on a cold cake.

Makes enough to cover one 8-inch-square cake.

BITTERSWEET CHOCOLATE FROSTING

3 ounces chocolate
(squares or envelopes)
3 tablespoons butter

½ cup milk
2 cups confectioners' sugar
(about)

Put the first three ingredients in a saucepan and stir over low heat until they are all blended. Do not boil. Add enough of the sugar to give the desired consistency. Stir and cook for a few minutes, then spread on a cold cake.

Makes about 2¼ cups.

BLACK AND WHITE PEPPERMINT FROSTING

Use this on your favorite devil's-food cake.

1½ cups sugar
5 tablespoons water
1 tablespoon corn syrup
2 egg whites

¼ teaspoon peppermint extract
1-ounce square chocolate, melted

1. Put sugar, water, corn syrup, and egg whites in the top of a double boiler. Stir until sugar is dissolved. Cook over boiling water, beating constantly, until the frosting is fluffy and forms peaks. Stir in the peppermint.

2. Frost top and sides of cake. Pour the melted chocolate in thin lines about 1 inch apart across the top of the frosting. Cross these lines with a wooden pick, giving a marbleized effect.

Makes enough to frost an 8-inch 2-layer cake.

BROILED ALMOND FROSTING

¼ cup butter, melted
½ cup firmly packed brown
sugar
2 tablespoons heavy cream

⅓ cup chopped toasted almonds
Few drops of almond extract

Mix all ingredients together well. Spread over cake.

Preheat broiler and place cake 3 inches away. Leave for a minute or two or until slightly brown.

Makes enough to frost a 9-inch-square cake.

Variation: Other nuts may be substituted for the almonds. In that case use 1 teaspoon vanilla extract instead of the almond extract.

CARAMEL FROSTING

This seems to have a special affinity for chocolate cake of any kind.

2 cups firmly packed
brown sugar
½ cup heavy cream

½ cup butter
1 teaspoon vanilla extract

1. Stir the sugar, cream, and butter over low heat until the sugar is dissolved. Cook without stirring to the soft ball stage (238° F. on a candy thermometer). Remove from the heat and cool to lukewarm (about 110° F.).

2. Add the vanilla and beat until of the proper consistency to spread.

Makes about 3 cups.

CARAMEL GLAZE

½ cup sugar
1 teaspoon lemon juice
½ cup water

⅝ cup firmly packed brown sugar

1. Cook the sugar and lemon juice over low heat until the syrup begins to turn golden. Add the water and sugar. Cook slowly until a candy thermometer reaches 290° F.

2. Pour the hot glaze over the cake and spread quickly with a hot spatula. Mark into serving pieces before the glaze hardens.

Makes enough to cover an 8- or 9-inch layer.

CHOCOLATE BUTTERCREAM ICING

¼ cup butter
¾ cup confectioners' sugar
1 teaspoon vanilla extract

3 ounces chocolate (envelopes or melted squares)
2 egg whites
Pinch of salt

1. Cream the butter and sugar together. Add the vanilla and the chocolate. Blend thoroughly.

2. Whip the egg whites with the salt until stiff. Fold these into the chocolate mixture.

Makes about 1½ cups.

CHOCOLATE BUTTER ICING

½ cup butter
1 cup confectioners' sugar
Few grains of salt
2 egg yolks

3 ounces chocolate (squares, melted and cooled, or envelopes)

Cream the butter. Add the sugar gradually, whipping until the frosting is light and fluffy. Add the salt. Add the egg yolks, beating in thoroughly. Blend in the chocolate. Spread on a cold cake.

Makes enough to cover an 8-inch-square cake.

CHOCOLATE CREAM-CHEESE ICING

Try this exceptionally smooth icing for something that is out of the ordinary.

3 ounces soft cream cheese	1 teaspoon vanilla extract
3 tablespoons heavy cream	Few grains of salt
2 cups confectioners' sugar	
2 ounces chocolate (squares, melted and cooled, or envelopes)	

Beat the cheese and cream well. Then add the confectioners' sugar, a little at a time, beating as you add. Mix in the chocolate, vanilla, and salt. Beat all together thoroughly and spread on the cake.

Makes enough to cover an 8- or 9-inch-square cake.

CHOCOLATE FONDANT GLAZE FOR PETITS FOURS

See recipe for Chocolate Fondant (p. 290).

Melt fondant in the top of a double boiler. If too thick, add hot water, a little at a time, or crème de cacao. Stir until of proper consistency.

Pour generously over *petits fours* on a cake rack set on a baking sheet. Any fondant that drips onto the baking sheet may be scraped up, melted, and used again.

Makes enough glaze for about 2 dozen *petits fours*, depending on their size.

CHOCOLATE FROSTING FOR TORTEN

4 ounces chocolate (squares, melted, or envelopes)	¾ cup water ½ cup sugar

Blend the chocolate and water over low heat. Add the sugar and bring to a boil. Cook for 8 minutes, or until the syrup spins a thread (238° F. on a candy thermometer). Remove from the heat and stir until the frosting thickens and is slightly cooled. Spread.

Makes about 1½ cups.

CHOCOLATE GLAZE

Use less sugar for a thin glaze to dribble over cake. A thicker glaze can be used to frost a cake or cupcakes.

3 tablespoons cocoa	1 tablespoon corn syrup
2 tablespoons water	1 cup (more or less) confectioners' sugar
1 tablespoon butter	

1. Mix cocoa, water, butter, and corn syrup. Cook over low heat, stirring while the mixture cooks, until it is smooth.

2. Remove from the heat. Stir in the amount of sugar necessary to make a glaze of the desired thickness.

Makes about 1½ cups.

CHOCOLATE GLAZE FOR COOKIES

Brush this on cookies after baking for an attractive finish.

1 ounce unsweetened choc-
olate (square, melted, or
envelope)

¾ cup confectioners' sugar

1 tablespoon hot milk

Mix all ingredients together. Add more milk if necessary to bring the glaze to the proper consistency.

Makes enough to glaze 15 to 20 cookies.

THIN CHOCOLATE GLAZE

⅓ cup sugar
¼ cup water

2 ounces chocolate
(squares, melted, or en-
velopes)
1 tablespoon butter
1 tablespoon milk

Boil the sugar and water for 1 minute, then pour over the chocolate. Add the butter and milk. Blend and cool. Pour the glaze over a cake and let it run down the sides.

Makes enough for one average-sized cake.

CHOCOLATE MARSHMALLOW FROSTING

2 cups sugar
½ cup water
2 egg whites

½ teaspoon cream of tartar
14 marshmallows
1 ounce square chocolate

1. Boil the sugar and water together until it spins a thread (238° F. on a candy thermometer).

Cake Fillings, Frostings, and Icings ◆ *109*

2. Beat the egg whites until frothy. Add the cream of tartar and beat until very stiff. Lay the marshmallows on the egg whites, and slowly pour the syrup over them, beating as you pour. When stiff enough, spread on the cake.

3. Melt the chocolate over hot water, and drizzle over the icing. Makes enough to frost a 3-layer cake.

CHOCOLATE ORANGE FROSTING

¼ cup butter
2 cups confectioners' sugar
2 teaspoons grated orange rind

2 ounces chocolate (squares, melted, or envelopes)
Pinch of salt
¼ cup orange juice

1. Cream the butter and add half of the sugar. Beat until light and creamy. Add the orange rind, chocolate, and salt. Add the rest of the sugar alternately with the orange juice.

2. Stir over low heat until the frosting is soft and creamy. Remove from the heat and spread on a cold cake.

Makes about 2½ cups.

CHOCOLATE RUM ICING

6 ounces chocolate (squares, melted, or envelopes)
6 tablespoons butter

5 cups confectioners' sugar (about)
Pinch of salt
¼ cup dark rum

1. Blend the chocolate and the butter in the top of a double boiler. Add 3 cups of the sugar and cook over boiling water for 5 minutes, stirring as the mixture cooks.

2. Remove from the heat and add the salt and rum. Stir in

enough additional sugar to give the icing the proper consistency for spreading.

Makes enough to ice three 9-inch layers.

CHOCOLATE SATIN ICING

¼ cup sugar	½ cup soft butter
2 tablespoons water	2 ounces chocolate
1 egg	(squares, melted, or en-
2⅓ cups confectioners'	velopes)
sugar	1 tablespoon vanilla ex-
	tract

1. Mix the sugar and water and bring to a boil. Boil for 1 minute. Cool the syrup.

2. Beat the egg well, and then beat in the sugar. Add the syrup, butter, chocolate, and vanilla. Beat thoroughly until smooth. Spread on a cold cake.

Makes about 3 cups.

CHOCOLATE SOUR-CREAM FROSTING

3 ounces chocolate	4½ cups confectioners'
(squares, melted, or en-	sugar
velopes)	Pinch of salt
3 tablespoons butter	2 teaspoons vanilla extract
¾ cup sour cream	

Blend the chocolate and the butter. Mix sour cream, sugar, and salt in a bowl. Beat. Add the chocolate and the vanilla. Beat until smooth. Spread on a cold cake.

Makes enough to frost a 2-layer cake on top and sides.

CHOCOLATE VELVET FROSTING

1 cup sugar	3 ounces chocolate
4 tablespoons cornstarch	(squares, melted, or en-
Pinch of salt	velopes)
1 cup boiling water	3 tablespoons butter
	1 teaspoon vanilla extract

1. Mix the sugar, cornstarch, and salt in a saucepan. Stir in the water slowly and cook over a low heat until the mixture is thick and smooth, stirring as it cooks. Stir in the chocolate and the butter.

2. Cook until thick enough to spread. Add vanilla and cool. Stir occasionally while the frosting is cooling to prevent formation of a crust.

Makes about 2½ cups.

CINNAMON ICING

½ cup butter	1 pound (3½ cups) con-
1 teaspoon vanilla extract	fectioners' sugar
1 egg yolk	1 teaspoon ground cinna-
	mon

1. Cream the butter with the vanilla and the egg yolk in a saucepan.

2. Stir in the sugar and cinnamon, and put the pan over very low heat. Stir and cook until the icing is soft and creamy.

3. If you find the icing a little stiff, you may add a little of the egg white to thin it. Spread on a cold cake.

While we like this icing on a chocolate cake especially, it is also very good on a spice cake.

Makes enough to ice two 9-inch layers.

COCOA COFFEE ICING

2 tablespoons unsalted but
  ter
1 cup firmly packed brown
  sugar
1 teaspoon vanilla extract

2 tablespoons cocoa
1 teaspoon instant coffee
  powder
3 tablespoons hot water

Cream the butter, sugar, and vanilla together. Mix the cocoa and coffee powder with the hot water. Blend all together and beat until smooth and creamy.

Makes enough to ice an 8-inch-square cake.

COCOA ICING

½ cup butter
¾ cup granulated sugar
½ teaspoon salt
 4 tablespoons cocoa

1 tablespoon vanilla ex-
  tract
3 egg whites
¾ cup confectioners' sugar

1. Cream the butter and granulated sugar together until light and fluffy. Add the salt, the cocoa, and vanilla.

2. Whip the egg whites until they are foamy. Add the confectioners' sugar gradually, beating as you add. When stiff, fold the two mixtures together. Refrigerate until stiff enough to spread.

Makes enough to ice two 8-inch layers.

COCOA PECAN FILLING OR FROSTING

Use this as a filling or frosting or both.

1 cup sugar
1 cup undiluted evaporated milk
1 egg, beaten
1 egg yolk
⅓ cup soft butter

⅓ cup cocoa
1 cup shredded or grated coconut
1 cup chopped pecans
1 tablespoon vanilla extract

1. Mix the sugar and evaporated milk together. Beat in the egg and the egg yolk. Then add the butter and cocoa. Stir over low heat until the mixture is thick and smooth.

2. Add the coconut, nuts, and vanilla. Cool before spreading.

Makes enough to cover two 9-inch layers.

COFFEE RUM AND BUTTER FROSTING

½ cup butter
1 pound (3½ cups) confectioners' sugar
1 teaspoon instant coffee powder

3 tablespoons hot milk
1 tablespoon dark rum

1. Cream the butter and the sugar together.

2. Dissolve the coffee powder in the hot milk. Add to the creamed mixture. Add the rum. Whip all together until smooth and creamy. Spread on a cold cake.

Makes enough to cover the tops and sides of two layers.

CREAMY CARAMEL FROSTING

2 cups brown sugar, firmly
packed
1 cup heavy cream

3 tablespoons butter
1 teaspoon vanilla extract

1. Stir sugar and cream over low heat until the mixture comes to a boil. Continue cooking until the soft-ball stage is reached (238° F. on a candy thermometer). Remove from the heat, add the butter, and cool to 110° F.

2. Add the vanilla, and beat until the frosting has the proper consistency to spread.

Makes enough to frost a 2-layer cake.

CREAMY CHOCOLATE FROSTING

1½ cups confectioners'
sugar
2 tablespoons hot water
2 ounces chocolate
(squares, melted, or en-
velopes)

4 tablespoons soft butter
1 teaspoon vanilla extract

Beat the sugar and water together, then add the chocolate, beating well. Add the butter and vanilla, beating until all is smooth and creamy.

This will cover the top and sides of a 9-inch-square cake.

Double the recipe for three round layers.

DARK MOCHA FROSTING

1¼ cups confectioners' sugar (about)
½ cup cocoa
2 tablespoons butter
½ teaspoon ground cinnamon

1 teaspoon instant coffee powder
Pinch of salt
2 tablespoons cream

1. Place all ingredients in a saucepan and cook, stirring, over low heat for 5 or 6 minutes. If not thick enough to spread, add a little more sugar.

2. Beat well and spread on a cold cake.

FLUFFY COCOA FROSTING

1 egg white
1 cup confectioners' sugar
¼ cup cocoa

2 teaspoons heavy cream
1 teaspoon melted butter
1 teaspoon vanilla extract

Beat the egg white until stiff but not dry. Mix the sugar and cocoa and beat slowly into the egg white. Beat in the cream and the butter. Add the vanilla and beat until the icing has the proper consistency to spread.

Makes enough to ice an 8-inch-square cake.

FLUFFY WALNUT ICING

This frosting is quick and easy, but should be spread just before serving, as it does not stand well. It is excellent on a spice cake as well as a chocolate cake.

2 egg whites
¾ cup confectioners' sugar
⅓ cup corn syrup

Pinch of salt
½ cup walnuts, finely chopped

Put all ingredients except the nuts in an electric mixer. Beat at high speed until icing stands in stiff peaks. This may take 5 minutes or so. Fold in the nuts and spread on the cake.

Makes enough to ice two 8-inch layers.

FRENCH FROSTING

This is especially suited to the French Chocolate Cake on page 44, but of course may be used on any other cake which calls for a chocolate frosting.

½ cup firmly packed brown sugar	2 cups confectioners' sugar (about)
½ cup water	Pinch of salt
3 tablespoons butter	1 teaspoon vanilla extract
2 ounces chocolate (squares, melted, or envelopes)	

1. Bring the brown sugar and water to a boil. Add the butter and chocolate and blend thoroughly.

2. Stir in the confectioners' sugar, using just enough to give the frosting the proper consistency to spread. Add salt and vanilla, beat well, and spread on a cold cake.

Makes enough to frost a 9-inch-square cake.

FUDGE FROSTING

This old standby cannot be improved upon.

4 tablespoons butter	2 ounces chocolate (squares, melted, or envelopes)
2 cups sugar	
½ cup milk	1 teaspoon vanilla extract

1. Mix butter, sugar, and milk in a saucepan and bring to a boil. Cook for 10 to 12 minutes, or until the syrup reaches the soft-ball stage (238° F. on a candy thermometer). Add the chocolate, remove from the heat, and cool to lukewarm. Add vanilla and beat until thick.

2. Spread immediately on a cold cake.

Makes about 2¾ cups.

GLOSSY CHOCOLATE FROSTING

This is very chocolatey, very rich, and very delicious. Use for cakes, éclairs, or cream puffs.

½ cup sugar	Pinch of salt
2 tablespoons cornstarch	3 tablespoons butter
½ cup water	1 teaspoon vanilla extract
2 ounces chocolate (squares, melted, or envelopes)	

Mix sugar and cornstarch well. Stir in the water and then the chocolate and salt. Cook over low heat, stirring until the mixture is smooth and thick. Add butter and vanilla; stir. Spread on a cake while the frosting is still warm.

Makes enough to cover the tops of two layers.

LACE SUGAR TOPPING

Place a paper lace doily over your cake and sift confectioners' sugar over it. Carefully remove the doily and you will have a charming sugar design to decorate the top. This is particularly handsome on a dark chocolate cake.

LEMON GLAZE

1 cup confectioners' sugar   Lemon juice to moisten
Grated rind of ½ lemon

Add just enough lemon juice to the sugar and grated rind to make the glaze spreadable. This is very tart and is a pleasant foil for a rich sweet cooky.

This will glaze 18 to 24 cookies.

MOCHA FROSTING

1⅔ cups confectioners'   6 tablespoons soft butter
sugar   Pinch of salt
1 tablespoon cocoa   1 teaspoon dark rum
1 teaspoon instant coffee
powder

Blend all ingredients except the rum in a saucepan. Stir over very low heat until the frosting is soft and creamy. Stir in the rum and spread immediately on a cold cake.

Makes enough to frost the top of one 9-inch layer or the top of an 8-inch-square cake.

Variation: MOCHA BROWN-SUGAR FROSTING

Substitute 1⅓ cups brown sugar for the confectioners' sugar.

ORANGE CHEESE ICING

3 ounces soft cream cheese   2 teaspoons lemon juice
1 tablespoon grated orange   3 cups confectioners' sugar
rind   Few grains of salt
2 teaspoons orange juice

Cake Fillings, Frostings, and Icings ◆ 119

Cream the cheese, which should be at room temperature, with the orange rind and the fruit juices. Add the confectioners' sugar and salt. Spread on a chocolate cake.

Makes enough to ice a 9-inch-square cake.

PEPPERMINT BUTTERCREAM

½ cup soft butter	¼ teaspoon peppermint extract
2 cups confectioners' sugar	
1 or more tablespoons cream	Few drops red coloring (optional)

Blend the first three ingredients. Stir over low heat until creamy. Add the peppermint.

Makes about ¾ cup.

RICH CHOCOLATE FROSTING

2 cups sugar	2 eggs
½ cup milk	1 teaspoon vanilla extract
4 ounces chocolate (squares or envelopes)	

1. Cook sugar, milk, and chocolate over direct heat until the mixture comes to a boil.

2. Beat the eggs well, and slowly pour the hot mixture over them, beating as you pour. Return to the heat for a minute or two. Then remove from the heat and beat until the frosting is thick. Add the vanilla, and spread on a cold cake.

Makes enough to frost a 2-layer cake or tops and sides of an 8- or 9-inch-square cake.

RICH MOCHA BUTTER FROSTING

6 ounces semisweet choco-
late

¼ cup water

1 teaspoon instant coffee
powder

1½ cups unsalted butter

1 tablespoon vanilla ex-
tract

4 egg yolks

¾ cup light corn syrup

1. Combine the chocolate, water, and coffee powder in a saucepan. Simmer until chocolate is melted. Stir to blend well. Cool.

2. Cream the butter with the vanilla.

3. Beat egg yolks until thick and lemon-colored.

4. Boil the corn syrup until is spins a thread (238° F. on a candy
thermometer). Pour in a thin stream onto the yolks, beating as
you pour. Beat until the mixture is thick. Cool.

5. Beat the syrup and egg-yolk mixture very slowly into the
butter, then add the chocolate mixture. Mix just until blended.

Makes enough to cover sides and tops of two layers.

ROSE ICING

2 cups confectioners' sugar

Few grains of salt

1 teaspoon rose flavoring

Hot water

Red food coloring

Mix the sugar, salt, and rose flavoring. Add enough hot water to
make a thick icing. Color a delicate pink. Stir this over very low
heat until it softens sufficiently to spread. Ice a cold cake.

Makes enough to cover an 8-inch-square cake or to ice one layer.

RUM GLAZE

Use this on the top of a cake, a Torte, *cookies, or anything you can think of. It is truly delicious.*

1 cup confectioners' sugar 2 tablespoons dark rum
1 tablespoon water

Stir the sugar and water over low heat until the sugar is dissolved. Add the rum, drop by drop, and continue to cook and stir until the syrup is thick. Spread immediately over the top and sides of a cake or *Torte*.

Makes enough to glaze one layer.

SHERRY ICING

This is easy to mix and has a delicate flavor all its own. It is fine on a chocolate cake.

⅓ cup soft butter   2 cups confectioners' sugar
1 egg white   1 tablespoon grated orange
1 tablespoon sherry   rind

Put all ingredients in the bowl of a mixer and beat until smooth.

Spread on a cold cake. You may sprinkle more orange rind on top if you wish.

Makes enough to ice a 9-inch-square cake.

SHINY FROSTING FOR ÉCLAIRS AND CREAM PUFFS

1½ ounces chocolate (squares, melted, or envelopes)
¾ cup confectioners' sugar
1 teaspoon corn syrup

Few grains of salt
2 tablespoons heavy cream
1 teaspoon butter
1 teaspoon vanilla extract

Put the chocolate, sugar, corn syrup, salt, cream, and butter in a saucepan. Stir over low heat. Allow the frosting to cook for a minute or two, then remove from the heat and add the vanilla.

Cool slightly, and frost the éclairs.

This will cover about 12 éclairs or cream puffs of average size.

SNOWDRIFT FROSTING

2 cups sugar
1 cup water
2 egg whites

Pinch of salt
⅛ teaspoon cream of tartar
1 teaspoon vanilla extract

1. Boil sugar and water until the syrup spins a thread (238° F. on a candy thermometer).

2. Beat egg whites with the salt until they are stiff, and then pour the syrup slowly onto them, beating as you pour. Add the cream of tartar and vanilla. Continue to beat until the frosting reaches the right consistency to spread.

Makes enough to frost a 2-layer cake.

Variation: We like this topped with a thin layer of melted chocolate. Spread the chocolate quickly on top of the frosting as soon as the frosting has set sufficiently. Put the cake in the refrigerator for the chocolate layer to harden.

VANILLA ICING I

2 tablespoons butter
2 cups confectioners' sugar
2 tablespoons water

1 teaspoon almond or vanilla extract or rose flavoring

Melt the butter over low heat. Blend in the sugar. Add the water and stir until warm and creamy. Remove from the heat, add the flavoring, and spread on a cold cake.

Makes enough to ice a 9-inch-square cake.

VANILLA ICING II

The egg white in this adds to its smoothness. Use it on a cake or a coffee cake.

¼ cup soft butter
1½ cups confectioners' sugar

1 egg white
1 teaspoon vanilla extract

Cream the butter and sugar together until the mixture is light and creamy. Add the unbeaten egg white and the vanilla, and continue to beat until the icing is thick. This will take 5 to 10 minutes.

Makes enough to ice an 8-inch-square cake or one coffee cake.

DECORATIONS FOR DESSERTS

CHOCOLATE CURLS

*T*HESE ARE easily made and add glamour to any dessert.

Use either sweet or semisweet chocolate at room temperature. Take a vegetable parer with a long narrow blade and dip it in hot water to warm it slightly. Run it along the smooth edge of a square of chocolate, and a smooth chocolate curl should result. If the chocolate chips, or does not curl smoothly, dip the parer in hot water again.

Running the parer over the smooth side of a bar of sweet milk chocolate produces a longer, wider curl than when the sweet or semisweet chocolate is used.

CHOCOLATE SHAVINGS

Using a sharp knife or a potato parer, pare thin shavings from a square of unsweetened or semisweet chocolate. Sprinkle over the top of an iced cake or a grasshopper pie.

CHOCOLATE CUTOUTS

These add a festive touch to a party cake or pie.

1 cup semisweet chocolate
 bits

2 tablespoons vegetable
 shortening

1. Lay out a piece of foil on a counter or table, or on a cooky sheet.

2. Melt the chocolate and shortening in the top of a double boiler. Spread evenly, about ¼ inch thick, on the foil and allow to set.

3. Cut with your fanciest cooky cutters. Or use your creative imagination and design your own shapes out of cardboard; place the cardboard on the chocolate and cut around the edge with a sharp knife.

CHOCOLATE LEAVES

These are easy to make and form a very effective decoration for a cake or a pudding.

2 dozen leaves (lilac leaves,
 large rose leaves, or any
 from shrubs such as
 mock-orange, are good)

1 teaspoon butter
2 ounces semisweet choco-
 late
 or
½ cup semisweet morsels

1. Wash and dry leaves.

2. Melt the butter with the chocolate over hot water.

3. Brush the chocolate on the underside of the leaves about ⅛ inch thick. Do not let the chocolate cover the edges as it will then be difficult to separate from the leaves. Refrigerate to harden.

4. Carefully peel off the leaves, and return the chocolate leaves to the refrigerator until ready to use.

Many attractive effects may be produced using angelica for stems, and glacéed cherries or cinnamon drops to simulate fruits or berries.

Decorations for Desserts ◆ *127*

CHOCOLATE HORNS

6 ounces semisweet chocolate   Confectioners' sugar

1. Mark 3-inch squares on wax paper.

2. Melt the chocolate over hot water, and spread 1 teaspoon melted chocolate evenly inside each square. Place in the refrigerator to harden.

3. Loosen chocolate from wax paper. Allow it to soften at room temperature. Roll up the paper and the chocolate with it. Return to refrigerator to harden. Peel off the paper when ready to use.

4. Dust with sifted confectioners' sugar.
Use to decorate desserts or to make French pastries look professional.

Makes about 8 to 10 horns.

CHOCOLATE SLABS FOR FRENCH PASTRIES

Semisweet chocolate

1. Put wax paper on a cooky sheet.

2. Melt chocolate over hot water and spread ⅛ inch thick on the wax paper. Cool.

3. When chocolate has set sufficiently, cut into squares to fit the sides of French pastries. The buttercream or other icing used on the pastries will keep the little slabs attached.

WHIPPED-CREAM ROSETTES

Whip heavy cream. Flavor it with vanilla, or a liqueur. Put the cream in a pastry bag fitted with a tube that will make rosettes. Pipe out the rosettes on a cooky sheet. Freeze them and store to use as needed to decorate desserts.

CREAM PUFFS, ÉCLAIRS, AND OTHER SMALL PASTRIES

CREAM-PUFF PASTE

This will make one dozen of this most delectable of all French pastries. The French call this uncooked mixture pâte à chou.

1 cup water	1 cup sifted flour
½ cup butter	4 eggs

1. Bring the water and butter to a full boil. Stir in the flour all at once. Beat over low heat until the mixture forms a ball and leaves the side of the pan.

2. Remove from the heat and beat in the eggs, one at a time, being sure that each one is entirely incorporated before adding the next.

CHOCOLATE ÉCLAIRS

1. Make cream-puff paste (above). Shape the éclairs with a large pastry tube or with 2 spoons, placing them about 3 inches apart on an ungreased cooky sheet. They should be about 4 inches by 1 inch.

2. Bake in a 400° F. oven for 45 minutes. Be sure they are dry, as an underdone éclair will fall when taken out of the oven.

3. Remove to cake rack to cool slowly. Fill with Mocha Pastry Cream (p. 100) and frost with Shiny Frosting for Éclairs (p. 123).

Makes 12 éclairs.

CREAM PUFFS

Follow the recipe for Cream-Puff Paste (p. 130).

1. Drop the mixture from a spoon onto an ungreased cooky sheet. Shape with a spoon.

2. Bake in a 400° F. oven for 45 minutes for the large size and 30 minutes for the small puffs. Be sure that they are dry, or they will fall when taken out of the oven. Cool slowly and fill.

3. Fill with Custard Cream Filling (p. 199) or Chocolate Pastry Cream II (p. 97), and ice with Glossy Chocolate Frosting (p. 118) or Shiny Frosting for Cream Puffs (p. 123). Or you may fill the puffs with Chocolate Ice Cream (pp. 165–167) and top with Blender Fudge Sauce (p. 200). Or fill with Chocolate Whipped Cream (p. 98) and either ice the tops or serve with fudge sauce.

Makes 8 large puffs or 12 to 18 small ones.

CREAM-PUFF PIE

1 cup water	1 cup sifted flour
½ cup butter	4 eggs
¼ teaspoon salt	

1. Bring the water, butter, and salt to a boil. Remove from the heat.

2. Put the flour in all at once. Stir. Return to the heat and continue to stir over low heat until the mixture forms a ball and leaves the side of the pan. Again remove from the heat.

3. Beat in the eggs, one at a time, being sure that each one is entirely incorporated before adding the next. Turn the mixture onto a buttered cooky sheet, spreading it out into a circle about 1 inch thick.

4. Bake in a 425° F. oven for 1 hour. The cream puff will puff and become a delicate brown. Turn the oven off and leave it there for 30 minutes. Remove from the oven and cool completely before filling.

5. Split the cream puff, and fill with any of these: Chocolate Custard Filling (pp. 95–96), Chocolate Whipped Cream (p. 98), Mocha Rum Butter Filling or Mocha Pastry Cream (p. 100), uncooked Chocolate Rum Filling (p. 97). The tops may be sprinkled with sifted confectioners' sugar or iced with Glossy Chocolate Frosting (p. 118) or Shiny Frosting for Éclairs (p. 123).

Makes 8 to 10 servings.

CROQUEMBOUCHE

This is a dramatic dessert, which could well serve as a centerpiece for a buffet table.

Pastry (p. 251) for 1-crust pie

Cream-Puff Paste (*pâte à chou*) (p. 130)

Chocolate Pastry Cream II (p. 97)

Coffee Syrup (p. 206)
or
Chocolate Syrup (p. 205)

2 tablespoons crème de cacao

Confectioners' sugar, sifted

1. Roll pastry to the desired size (about a 9- or 10-inch circle is about right) and bake on a buttered cooky sheet in a 425° F. oven for 15 minutes, or until it begins to brown.

2. Make the *pâte à chou* and shape it into tiny cream puffs on a buttered baking sheet. There should be about 24 of them. Bake these in a 425° F. oven for 10 minutes, then at 350° F. for 10 to 15 minutes longer, or until the puffs are brown. If taken out of the oven too soon, they will fall. Cool on a cake rack. Fill with Chocolate Pastry Cream.

3. Make Coffee Syrup or Chocolate Syrup, add the liqueur, and dip the puffs quickly into the hot syrup. Arrange the puffs in a circle on the cooled pastry. Fill the center with the puffs, and

then pile them up so that they form a pyramid. Drizzle any left-over syrup over the top. Sift confectioners' sugar over this. Chill before serving.

Use a serving spoon and fork to serve.

Makes 12 to 24 servings.

ITALIAN CREAM PUFFS

This is the usual cream puff except for the addition of orange and lemon peels, and the filling is different, for it is that delicious combination of ricotta cheese and chocolate.

1. Follow the recipe for *pâte à chou* (Cream-Puff Paste, p. 130). Add to the paste

1 tablespoon sugar	1 teaspoon grated lemon rind
1 teaspoon grated orange rind	

2. Shape the puffs, bake and cool.

Filling

1 pound ricotta (Italian cottage cheese)	1 tablespoon grated orange rind
1 ounce unsweetened chocolate, grated	4 tablespoons sugar
	1 teaspoon almond extract
	2 or 3 tablespoons milk

1. Whip all the ingredients together, adding just enough milk to make the mixture as thick as a custard. It should not be runny.

2. Cool the puffs. Open them at the bottom and fill them. These may be dusted with confectioners' sugar; however, I recommend Glossy Chocolate Frosting (p. 118).

Makes about 8 servings.

PROFITEROLES

An elegant dessert, not too hard to make.

Cream-Puff Paste (p. 130)   Vanilla or chocolate ice
cream

1. Shape the cream-puff batter into tiny puffs, about 2 dozen. Bake in a 425° F. oven for 10 to 15 minutes, or until they puff and brown. Cool.

2. Fill with ice cream, and spoon Chocolate Sauce on top. Allow 4 or 5 puffs for each serving.

Makes 6 servings.

PRUNE PASTRIES

12 dried prunes	Pinch of salt
12 blanched almonds	½ cup vegetable shortening
1 cup flour	Dry white wine
1 teaspoon granulated sugar	Confectioners' sugar
	Cocoa

1. Soak or simmer the prunes until plumped and tender, and remove the pits and replace with almonds. Or use pitted ready-to-eat prunes.

2. Mix the flour, granulated sugar, and salt. Cut in the shortening with a pastry blender. Moisten with just enough wine to make the mixture hold together. Roll out and cut pastry into squares; put a prune in each one, and fold over. Press the edges together with a fork, and put on an ungreased cooky sheet.

Bake in a 375° F. oven for 30 minutes or until the pastry is brown. Roll immediately in confectioners' sugar mixed with cocoa. Serve hot.

Makes 12 snacks, good for nibbling at any time.

PANCAKES, WAFFLES, AND DOUGHNUTS

CHOCOLATE NUT PANCAKES

This interesting recipe is Russian in origin.

1 egg
2 egg yolks
1 cup cream
½ cup granulated sugar
2 teaspoons grated lemon rind
⅓ cup cocoa

1 cup flour
1 cup ground toasted almonds
4 tablespoons butter, melted
Confectioners' sugar

1. Beat the egg and egg yolks until thick and lemon-colored. Add the cream and granulated sugar and beat again. Add the lemon rind.

2. Sift the cocoa and flour together and mix in the almonds. Stir this and the melted butter into the egg mixture.

3. Spoon a little of the batter on a buttered griddle for each pancake. When lightly browned, turn, and brown the other side.

4. Roll up and sift confectioners' sugar over the top.

Makes 14 to 16 small pancakes.

CHOCOLATE PANCAKE DESSERT

¼ cup almonds
¼ cup seedless raisins
2 tablespoons brandy
4 eggs, separated
2 tablespoons cocoa
2 tablespoons cornstarch

½ teaspoon salt
1 tablespoon granulated sugar
½ cup lukewarm milk
Confectioners' sugar

1. Put the nuts and raisins through an electric blender with the brandy; or grind finely and add brandy. Set aside.

2. Beat the egg yolks well. Mix the cocoa, cornstarch, salt, and granulated sugar. Stir in the milk. Blend. Beat into the egg yolks. Beat egg whites stiff and fold into the first mixture.

3. Heat a large skillet. Butter it unless it is made of stickproof material. Pour in all the pancake batter and cook it over medium heat until done. This should take 5 to 7 minutes. Remove from heat.

4. Spread the nut-raisin mixture on top, roll up, and transfer to a warm serving dish. Dust confectioners' sugar over the top and serve.

Makes 2 servings.

FRENCH PANCAKES WITH CHOCOLATE SAUCE

This is the traditional recipe for crêpes. *After mixing, the batter should stand for 2 hours before cooking.*

⅔ cup flour
1 tablespoon sugar
Pinch of salt
2 whole eggs
2 extra egg yolks
1⅓ cups milk

2 tablespoons melted butter
1 tablespoon brandy
Confectioners' sugar, sifted
Apricot jam (optional)
Bittersweet Chocolate Sauce II (p. 199)

1. Sift the flour, sugar, and salt together.

2. Beat the whole eggs and the egg yolks well. Add the milk, and dry ingredients and beat until smooth. Add and mix in the butter and brandy. Set in refrigerator until needed.

3. *Crêpes* are traditionally cooked one at a time in a small frying pan. (I use an electric griddle, which does very well and has the advantage of allowing several to be cooked at once.) Butter the frying pan, pour in a small amount of batter, and spread it thinly, tilting the pan so that the batter is evenly spread. Cook for about 1 minute, turn, and cook the other side.

Dust tops lightly with confectioners' sugar. Set aside and keep warm.

To serve, stack pancakes on top of each other, spreading each thinly with warm jam, cut into wedges, and pass Chocolate Sauce.

Makes about 14 small pancakes.

CHOCOLATE WAFFLES

½ cup butter
1 cup sugar
2 eggs
1 teaspoon vanilla extract
2½ ounces chocolate
    (squares, melted and
    cooled, or envelopes)

1½ cups sifted flour
2 teaspoons baking powder
¼ teaspoon salt
Dash of ground cinnamon
½ cup milk
Ice cream
Rum Sauce (p. 204)

1. Cream the butter and sugar well. Add the eggs, one at a time, beating after each addition. Beat in the vanilla and the chocolate.

2. Sift the flour, baking powder, salt, and cinnamon together, and add to the creamed mixture alternately with the milk.

3. Bake in a preheated waffle iron, following the directions given with the appliance.

Serve hot with a scoop of ice cream. We can't resist passing hot Rum Sauce to go on top.

Makes 6 servings.

CHOCOLATE DOUGHNUTS

Eat fresh and hot with steaming fragrant coffee, or dunk in milk—a treat either way.

½ cup butter
1 cup granulated sugar
2 eggs
1½ ounces chocolate
  (squares, melted and
  cooled, or envelopes)
4 cups sifted flour
2 teaspoons baking powder

1 teaspoon salt
¼ teaspoon ground cinna-
  mon
1 cup milk
½ teaspoon vanilla extract
  Confectioners' sugar
  Cocoa

1. Cream the butter and granulated sugar until light and fluffy. Add the eggs, one at a time, beating well after each addition. Stir in the cooled chocolate.

2. Sift the flour, baking powder, salt, and cinnamon together and add alternately with the milk. Add the vanilla.

3. Roll out on a lightly floured board and cut with a doughnut cutter. Fry in deep fat at 365° F. on a frying thermometer for 1½ minutes. Then turn the doughnuts and fry for another 1½ minutes.

4. Drain on paper towels. Sprinkle with confectioners' sugar mixed with cocoa.

Makes 2 dozen.

Variation: CHOCOLATE SPICE DOUGHNUTS

Add 1 teaspoon ground cinnamon and ½ teaspoon freshly grated nutmeg to the dry ingredients. Dust with cinnamon-sugar.

FRUITS WITH CHOCOLATE

CHOCOLATE APPLE BETTY

¼ cup butter
½ cup fine bread crumbs
¼ cup firmly packed brown
  sugar

3 cups sliced tart apples
Water
4 ounces chocolate, grated
Vanilla ice cream

1. Butter a 1-quart casserole or baking dish of any kind.

2. Melt the butter, add the crumbs, and stir over low heat until the crumbs are slightly brown. Mix in the sugar.

3. Simmer the apples in a little water until they are soft. Arrange in layers with the crumb mixture, ending with crumbs on top. Sprinkle the grated chocolate on top of that.

4. Bake in a 325° F. oven for 30 minutes. Chill.

5. Serve cold with ice cream on top.

Makes 4 to 6 servings.

CHOCOLATE APPLE SLICES

1 cup sugar
1 cup honey
1 teaspoon ground cinna-
  mon
½ cup water

Few grains of salt
3 firm apples
8 ounces semisweet choco-
  late

1. Put sugar, honey, cinnamon, water, and salt in a saucepan, bring to a boil, and boil for 5 minutes.

2. Core and peel the apples. Cut them into slices about ½-inch thick. Drop the slices into the boiling syrup and cook until the apples are transparent. The syrup will have practically cooked away. Place slices on a cake rack to drain and dry.

3. Melt the chocolate over hot water, and carefully dip each apple slice into it. Place them on wax paper to dry.

Makes 12 to 15 slices.

CHOCOLATE TIDBITS

A delightful and different way to end a meal. Serve this in the living room with coffee and liqueurs.

2 cups Rich Chocolate Sauce (pp. 201–202)
2 tablespoons cognac
Glacéed cherries
Glacéed pineapple
Squares of fruitcake
Candied orange peel

Canned pineapple chunks
Dates, pitted and cut into halves
Maraschino cherries
Figs, cut into bite-size pieces

1. Mix the Chocolate Sauce and cognac. Place in a heatproof dish over a coffee warmer to keep warm, but don't let it get too hot.

2. Arrange a tray of tidbits, with a cocktail pick in each one so that guests can dip the tidbits of their choice into the warm sauce. A "do-it-yourself" dessert.

The list of tidbits is merely a suggestion. Many others may be added as, of course, anything is delicious encased in chocolate.

CHOCOLATE TRIFLE WITH FRESH RASPBERRIES

6 slices of chocolate cake
4 tablespoons dark rum
1 quart raspberries

Sugar
2 cups heavy cream
1 tablespoon rosewater

1. For the chocolate cake, use Cocoa Spongecake (p. 60) or make or buy a chocolate loaf cake; in any case, the cake should be several days old. Arrange the cake slices on a serving platter. Sprinkle with rum.

2. Wash and drain raspberries (reserving a few perfect berries to decorate the trifle when completed). Sweeten them to taste and let them stand.

3. Whip the cream and fold in the rosewater and the raspberries. Spoon this over the cake. Decorate with strawberry or grape leaves, and the raspberries reserved for this purpose.

Serve immediately.

Makes 6 servings.

ORANGE FRITTERS WITH ORANGE CHOCOLATE SAUCE

4 oranges
2 cups granulated sugar
2 cups water
1¼ cups dry white wine
3 tablespoons melted butter

1¼ cups sifted flour
3 egg whites
Confectioners' sugar, sifted
Orange Chocolate Sauce (pp. 202–203)

1. Peel the oranges and remove the sections, discarding seeds and membrane.

2. Boil the granulated sugar and water to make a syrup, and marinate the orange sections in this for an hour or two. Drain them.

3. Stir the wine and butter into the flour, beating until smooth.

4. Beat the egg whites until stiff and gently fold into the batter. Dip the orange sections into the batter, and fry in deep fat at 370° F. for a minute or two, or until the fritters are a delicate brown.

5. Drain the fritters on paper toweling, dust them with confectioners' sugar, and serve piping hot with Orange Chocolate Sauce.

Makes 6 to 8 servings.

PÊCHES PARISIENNE

A delightfully different dessert that everyone will enjoy.

6 ripe peaches
1½ cups water
½ cup sugar
Few drops of almond extract

6 slices of spongecake
2 ounces (4 tablespoons) Benedictine
Blender Fudge Sauce (p. 200)

1. Peel and halve the peaches. Simmer them in a syrup made of the water, sugar, and almond extract. Cool the fruit in the syrup, and drain.

2. Arrange the slices of spongecake on dessert plates. Sprinkle Benedictine over the cake. Place the peaches on top, and serve with Blender Fudge Sauce.

Makes 6 servings.

PEARS WITH CHOCOLATE

1¼ cups sugar
2 cups water
1 teaspoon vanilla extract
8 pears

4 ounces chocolate (squares, melted, or envelopes)
1 tablespoon butter

1. Make a syrup by boiling the sugar and water together for 5 minutes. Add the vanilla.

2. Peel, core, and slice the pears. Poach them in the syrup until they are tender. Lift them from the syrup with a slotted spoon and put them in a serving bowl.

3. Add the chocolate and butter to the syrup, and stir over low heat until well blended. Pour over the pears and chill.

Serve over vanilla ice cream.

Makes 8 servings.

PUDDINGS

BAKED CHOCOLATE CREAM

½ cup butter
1 cup confectioners' sugar
1 teaspoon vanilla extract
6 eggs, separated
6 ounces unsweetened chocolate (squares, melted and cooled, or envelopes)
1 cup light cream
1 cup milk
5 tablespoons cornstarch, mixed with the milk
Rum Sauce (p. 204)

1. Butter a 1½-quart pudding dish.

2. Cream the butter and sugar until smooth. Add the vanilla, then the egg yolks, one at a time, beating after each addition. Stir in the cooled chocolate, the mixed cornstarch and milk, and the cream.

3. Beat the egg whites until stiff and fold them into the pudding. Pour into the prepared dish, and set the dish into a pan of hot water.

Bake in a 350° F. oven for 45 minutes.

Serve warm with Rum Sauce.

Makes 6 to 8 servings.

BAKED CHOCOLATE CUSTARD

3 cups milk or half-and-half
2 ounces chocolate (squares, cut up, or envelopes)
5 eggs
⅓ cup of sugar
¼ teaspoon salt
1 teaspoon vanilla extract
Freshly grated nutmeg

1. Put the milk and chocolate in the top of a double boiler. Stir and cook over gently boiling water until they are blended.

2. Beat the eggs, sugar, salt, and vanilla well. Pour the hot chocolate mixture over this slowly, stirring as you pour. Turn into a buttered 1½-quart baking dish, and set the dish in a pan of hot water. Grate nutmeg on the top.

3. Bake in a 350° F. oven for 40 to 50 minutes, or until the custard is set on the edges; or test by inserting a knife in the custard. If the knife comes out clean, it is done. The custard will continue to cook a little after it comes out of the oven, so the center should not be quite set when it is removed.

Serve warm or cold. Top with whipped cream if you like.

Makes 4 to 6 servings.

Variation: BAKED MOCHA CUSTARD

Substitute ¼ cup honey for the sugar and add 1 teaspoon instant coffee powder to the chocolate and milk.

BITTERSWEET CHOCOLATE MOUSSE

5 ounces chocolate (squares or envelopes)	8 egg yolks
4 ounces semisweet chocolate	1⅓ cups sugar
	1 quart heavy cream
	2 tablespoons dark rum

1. Melt both kinds of chocolate over hot water.

2. Beat the egg yolks until they are thick and lemon-colored. Add the sugar while you continue to beat. When the mixture is thick and smooth, fold in the chocolate. Cool.

3. Whip the cream until stiff and fold it into the chocolate mixture together with the rum. Run in an electric mixer at low speed for a few seconds for perfect blending.

4. Spoon into serving dish and chill.

Makes 10 to 12 servings.

Note: This freezes well.

BOILED CHOCOLATE CUSTARD

This may be served as a dessert or used as a sauce on cake or pudding.

2 ounces chocolate (squares, cut up, or envelopes)	4 egg yolks
	½ cup sugar
	Pinch of salt
2 cups milk	1 teaspoon vanilla extract

1. Heat the chocolate and milk over low heat until the two are hot and blended.

2. Beat the egg yolks with the sugar and salt. Add the hot liquid slowly, stirring as you add.

3. Cook over low heat or in the top of a double boiler over simmering water until the custard coats the spoon. It will not get very thick.

4. Cool and add the vanilla. Chill.

Makes 4 to 6 servings as a pudding.

Variations: CHOCOLATE FLOATING ISLAND

Boiled Chocolate Custard (recipe above)	2 tablespoons sugar
	2 tablespoons cocoa
1 egg white	1 teaspoon vanilla extract

1. Pour the custard into a serving bowl. Chill.

2. Beat the egg white stiff and gradually add the sugar and cocoa which have been mixed together. Beat until peaks are formed. Stir in the vanilla and spoon over the custard.

CHOCOLATE BREAD PUDDING

An old-time favorite, with orange rind to add a pleasant contrast.

2 cups milk
2 ounces unsweetened chocolate (squares, cut up, or envelopes)
3 cups stale bread, cubed (no crusts)

½ cup sugar
Pinch of salt
3 egg yolks
1 tablespoon grated orange rind
1 teaspoon vanilla extract

1. Butter a 2-quart soufflé dish or pudding dish.

2. Combine the milk and the chocolate. Stir over low heat until well blended. Pour this over the bread and allow it to soak till mixture below is ready.

3. Beat the sugar, salt, egg yolks, orange rind, and vanilla together. Stir this slowly into the chocolate-bread mixture. Pour the pudding into the prepared dish, and set the dish in a pan of hot water.

4. Bake in a 350° F. oven for 45 minutes, or until set. Serve warm or cold with plenty of heavy cream.

Makes 6 servings.

CHOCOLATE LIQUEUR CREAM

4 eggs, separated
8 tablespoons (½ cup) sugar
4 ounces chocolate (squares, melted and cooled, or envelopes)

½ cup heavy cream
2 tablespoons crème de cacao
4 tablespoons Tia Maria

1. Beat the egg yolks well, and add 4 tablespoons of the sugar. Beat until light and creamy. Beat in the chocolate, and then the cream. Cook over hot water, stirring while the mixture cooks, until it thickens. Cool slightly.

2. Whip the egg whites until they are stiff, and then beat in the other 4 tablespoons of sugar. Fold this meringue carefully into the chocolate mixture. Now fold in the liqueurs. Place the liqueur cream in the refrigerator to chill thoroughly.

To serve, spoon into parfait glasses, decorate with a swirl of whipped cream, and top with a candied violet.

Makes 8 servings.

CHOCOLATE LIQUEUR CREAM PUDDING

Boiled Chocolate Custard (p. 150)
1 cup heavy cream

Crème de cacao
Chocolate Curls (p. 126)

1. Pour cold chocolate custard into a serving bowl.

2. Whip the cream, add crème de cacao to taste, and spoon the cream over the custard. Decorate with Chocolate Curls.

CHOCOLATE MERINGUE TRIFLE

This is delicious served warm or cold.

6 slices stale spongecake
Orange marmalade
Chocolate Pastry Cream I (pp. 96–97)
2 teaspoons grated orange rind

2 egg whites
2 tablespoons sugar
1 teaspoon lemon juice

1. Butter a 2-quart soufflé dish. Arrange the cake slices in the bottom. Spread orange marmalade on the cake.

2. Make the Chocolate Pastry Cream, adding the orange rind. Spoon this over the cake.

3. Make a meringue by beating the egg whites until stiff and adding the sugar slowly while you continue to beat. Add the lemon juice. Beat until stiff peaks are formed. Spoon the meringue on the pudding.

Bake in a 325° F. oven until the meringue is slightly brown, which should take about 10 minutes.

Makes 6 servings.

CHOCOLATE NUT SPONGE

This is a different kind of a steamed pudding; it is light and delicate.

5 egg whites	½ cup nuts, ground or put
Pinch of salt	through a blender
½ cup sugar	1 teaspoon vanilla extract
2 ounces chocolate	
(squares, melted and	
cooled, or envelopes)	

1. Beat the egg whites with the salt until stiff. Gradually beat in the sugar. Gently fold the cooled chocolate and then the nuts into the meringue. Add the vanilla.

2. Cook, covered, in the buttered top of a double boiler, over, not in, boiling water for 45 minutes.

Serve warm with heavy cream or chocolate sauce.

Makes 4 servings.

CHOCOLATE SOUFFLÉ

3 tablespoons butter	4 eggs, separated
2 tablespoons flour	1 extra egg white
1 cup milk	1 teaspoon vanilla extract
½ cup sugar	Pinch of salt
3 ounces unsweetened chocolate (squares, melted, or envelopes)	1 tablespoon bourbon whiskey
	Chantilly Cream (p. 95)

1. Butter a 2-quart soufflé dish and sprinkle it with sugar. (You may fasten a foil collar around the dish so that the soufflé will rise higher.)

2. Melt the butter, stir in the flour, and then the milk. Cook, stirring, until thick and smooth. Add the sugar and the chocolate. Mix well.

3. Beat the egg yolks, and slowly beat in the hot chocolate mixture. Return to the heat and cook for a minute longer. Remove from the heat and add the vanilla, salt, and the bourbon.

4. Whip all five egg whites stiff, and fold into the chocolate mixture. Pour into the prepared dish, and set the dish in a pan of hot water.

5. Bake in a 350° F. oven for 40 minutes. Serve immediately with Chantilly Cream.

Makes 4 to 6 servings.

CHOCOLATE VELVET

Make this the day before for the peak of flavor to develop.

6 ounces chocolate (squares, melted, or envelopes)	2 tablespoons Chokaulu liqueur
4 tablespoons honey	Few grains of salt
¼ cup hot strong coffee	1 cup heavy cream, whipped
4 eggs, separated	

1. Stir the chocolate, honey, and coffee over low heat until well blended. Cool slightly. Stir in 1 egg yolk at a time, mixing well. Add the liqueur.

2. Whip the egg whites with the salt until stiff. Fold the chocolate mixture into the egg whites carefully but thoroughly.

3. Whip the cream and fold into the pudding. Chill.

Makes 6 servings.

CHOCOLATE WALNUT PUDDING

6 eggs	Pinch of salt
1 cup sugar	1 cup ground walnuts
2 ounces chocolate (squares, melted and cooled, or envelopes)	1 teaspoon vanilla extract

1. Beat the eggs until they are creamy and light in color. Beat in the sugar gradually. Add the chocolate, salt, walnuts, and vanilla. Spread in a shallow buttered baking dish.

Bake in a 250° F. oven until set, which will take 20 to 30 minutes.

To serve, top with whipped cream or ice cream.

Makes 4 servings.

CHOKALU CUSTARD

A dessert that can be served with pride on any important occasion.

6 egg yolks	3 cups light cream
¼ cup sugar	½ cup mixed candied fruits
2 tablespoons Chokalu liqueur	Whipped cream
Pinch of salt	Chocolate Curls (p. 126)

1. Place the egg yolks in the top of a double boiler. Beat. Add the sugar, liqueur, and salt. Mix well.

2. Scald the cream, and slowly pour over the egg-yolk mixture, stirring as you pour. Cook in double boiler over hot water, stirring, until the custard coats the spoon. Stir in the fruit. Pour into individual serving dishes. Chill.

To serve, top with a swirl of whipped cream, decorated with Chocolate Curls.

Makes 6 servings.

CRÈME DE CACAO SOUFFLÉ

3 tablespoons butter	¼ cup sugar
4 tablespoons flour	1 extra egg white
1 cup milk	¼ cup crème de cacao
4 eggs, separated	

1. Butter a 1-quart soufflé dish on the bottom only.

2. Melt the butter, stir in the flour, and cook for a minute or two. Add the milk and stir over low heat until the sauce is thick and smooth.

3. Beat the egg yolks until thick and lemon-colored. Beat in the sugar. Stir in the hot mixture slowly, beating as you add.

4. Beat the egg whites until stiff but not dry. Fold into the egg-yolk mixture. Add the crème de cacao and pour into the soufflé dish.

Bake in a 375° F. oven for 45 to 55 minutes, or until it is done.

Test with a silver knife. Serve immediately. Pass chocolate sauce.

Makes 4 to 6 servings.

DUTCH CHOCOLATE PUDDING

4 tablespoons Dutch cocoa	2 cups milk
4 tablespoons cornstarch	1 tablespoon butter
6 tablespoons sugar	1 teaspoon vanilla extract
Few grains of salt	

1. Combine cocoa, cornstarch, sugar, and salt. Stir in ¼ cup of the milk and mix until smooth.

2. Heat remaining milk, and stir into the first mixture.

3. Cook in the top of a double boiler over boiling water, stirring, until the pudding is thick. Continue to cook for 10 minutes, stirring occasionally. Remove from heat, stir in the butter and then the vanilla. Pour into individual custard cups or serving dishes. Chill.

Serve with heavy cream, plain or whipped.

Makes 4 servings.

PARFAIT PARISIENNE

3 eggs, separated	½ teaspoon vanilla extract
2 ounces choclate (squares, melted and cooled, or envelopes)	1 cup heavy cream, whipped
1 cup sugar	Grated orange rind (optional)

1. Beat the egg yolks until thick and creamy. Beat in the chocolate, and then the sugar.

2. Whip the egg whites until stiff. Fold into the chocolate mixture.

To serve: Spoon the chocolate mixture into parfait glasses, alternating with the whipped cream flavored with the vanilla, and ending with cream on top. A little grated orange rind is good on this.

Makes 4 servings.

POTS-DE-CRÈME AU CHOCOLAT I

There is absolutely nothing more delectable than this traditional French custard.

2 cups rich milk	6 egg yolks
½ pound semisweet chocolate bits	2 tablespoons brandy

1. Butter 8 *pot-de-crème* cups or other custard cups.

2. Stir the milk and the chocolate together over medium heat until thick and smooth.

3. Beat egg yolks until thick and creamy. Slowly add the chocolate milk mixture, beating as you add. Beat until it is slightly cool. Mix in the brandy. Strain into the *pot-de-crème* cups. Chill in the refrigerator until firm.

Makes 8 servings.

POTS-DE-CRÈME AU CHOCOLAT II

3 egg yolks	6 ounces semisweet chocolate bits
2 tablespoons sugar	
Pinch of salt	1 tablespoon butter
1¼ cups milk	1 teaspoon vanilla extract

1. Beat the egg yolks, sugar, and salt together. Add the milk and cook and stir over boiling water for 5 minutes. Add the chocolate bits, butter, and vanilla. Stir over boiling water until the chocolate is melted and all is well blended.

2. Pour into *pot-de-crème* cups or other custard cups. Chill thoroughly in refrigerator.

Makes 4 servings.

POTS-DE-CRÈME AU CHOCOLAT III

3 cups heavy cream	8 egg yolks
4 ounces chocolate (squares, cut up, or envelopes)	2 teaspoons vanilla extract
	Few grains of salt
⅓ cup sugar	Heavy cream, whipped

1. Butter a 6-cup soufflé dish or 12 individual custard cups.

2. Cook the cream, chocolate, and sugar over low heat until all is blended. Cool slightly.

3. Beat the egg yolks, and add the chocolate mixture very slowly, beating as you add. Stir in the vanilla and salt. Strain the pudding into the prepared cups or dish, and set them in a pan of hot water.

Bake in a 325° F. oven for 25 minutes—longer if a single baking dish is used—or until set around the edges. Chill.

Serve cold with slightly sweetened whipped cream.

Makes 10 to 12 servings.

Variation: POT-DE-CRÈME PIE

Make a Chocolate-Wafer Crust (p. 253). Fill the cooled crust with a filling made from any recipe for *Pots-de-Crème au Chocolat.*

RICH CHOCOLATE BLANCMANGE

3 egg yolks	2 ounces chocolate (squares, cut up, or envelopes)
½ cup sugar	
2 tablespoons flour	
Pinch of salt	1 tablespoon vanilla extract
2 cups rich milk	

1. Beat the egg yolks well. Beat in the sugar and the flour, mixed. Add the salt. Stir in the milk and add the chocolate and cook in the top of a double boiler over simmering water until the pudding is thick and smooth. Add the vanilla.

3. Spoon into a serving bowl and chill. Serve with cream, whipped or plain.

Makes 6 servings.

STEAMED ALMOND PUDDING WITH HONEY CHOCOLATE SAUCE

6 tablespoons butter	½ cup ground almonds
3 tablespoons sugar	½ teaspoon almond extract
3 eggs, separated	Honey Chocolate Sauce
3 tablespoons flour	(p. 202)
Pinch of salt	

1. Butter a 1-quart pudding dish.

2. Cream the butter and sugar together. Add the egg yolks, one at a time, beating well after each addition.

3. Beat the egg whites until they are stiff but not dry, and fold these into the first mixture alternately with the flour and salt. Fold in the nuts and flavoring. Pour into the prepared dish.

4. Place the pudding dish in a steamer and steam for 1 hour. Serve warm with Honey Chocolate Sauce (p. 202).

Makes 4 servings.

STEAMED CHOCOLATE PUDDING

2 tablespoons melted butter	1½ cups sifted flour
⅔ cup sugar	1 teaspoon salt
2 eggs	¼ teaspoon baking soda
3 ounces chocolate (squares, melted and cooled, or envelopes)	¼ teaspoon cream of tartar
	1 cup milk
	Whipped cream
1 teaspoon vanilla extract	Rum Sauce (p. 204)

1. Butter a 1-quart pudding mold.

2. Cream the butter and sugar together. Beat in the eggs, one at a time, beating after each addition. Then beat in the cooled chocolate and the vanilla.

3. Sift the flour, salt, baking soda, and cream of tartar together and beat this into the chocolate mixture alternately with the milk.

4. Pour into the prepared mold. Steam for 2 hours.

To serve, unmold and surround the base of the pudding with whipped cream. We like to pass Rum Sauce with this.

Makes 8 servings.

FROZEN DESSERTS

BOMBES

*T*HESE attractive desserts retain the glamour of bygone days, and are a fitting ending to a memorable meal. With modern refrigeration they are easy to make and a delight to serve.

Line a melon mold with a rather rich ice cream. Press it firmly onto the sides. Return it to the freezer for a short time if necessary. Fill the center with any ice cream or sherbet having a contrasting color and flavor.

Here are some good combinations: *Serve with:*

French Chocolate Ice Cream (pp. 165–166) Pistachio Parfait	Blender Fudge Sauce, hot (p. 200)
Coffee Ice Cream Frozen Chocolate Fruit Pudding (p. 170)	Honey Chocolate Sauce (p. 202)
French Vanilla Ice Cream Thin Layer of Philadelphia Chocolate Ice Cream (p. 166) Raspberry Sherbet	Chocolate Sauce with Cointreau (p. 201)

Bittersweet Chocolate Mousse
 (p. 149)
Macaroon Bisque

Brown-Sugar Sherry
 Sauce (p. 200)

Frozen Chocolate Mousse
 (pp. 170–171)
Liqueur Sherbet (p. 173)

Rich Chocolate Sauce
 (p. 201)

Use your imagination to create other delectable combinations.

CHOCOLATE CHIP ICE CREAM

1 egg, separated
¼ cup sugar
1 teaspoon vanilla extract

1 cup heavy cream,
 whipped
3 ounces semisweet choco-
 late, grated

1. Beat the egg yolk. Add the sugar gradually, then the vanilla. Beat until smooth and creamy.

2. Beat the egg white until stiff and fold into the egg-yolk mixture. Fold in the whipped cream and the grated chocolate. Pour into refrigerator tray and freeze.

Makes 1 pint.

FRENCH CHOCOLATE ICE CREAM

6 ounces semisweet choco-
 late
2 tablespoons hot water
½ cup sugar
¼ cup water
 Pinch of salt

½ teaspoon cream of tartar
4 egg yolks
3 cups heavy cream
1 tablespoon vanilla ex-
 tract

1. Melt the chocolate over hot water, blending it with the 2 tablespoons hot water as it melts.

2. Boil the sugar, water, salt, and cream of tartar until the syrup forms a thread. This will be about 238° F. on a candy thermometer.

3. Beat the egg yolks until they are thick and lemon-colored. Pour the syrup onto them very slowly, beating as you pour. Beat in the chocolate mixture and add the heavy cream and vanilla, stirring until all is well blended.

4. Freeze in an old-fashioned freezer, or in a refrigerator tray. If the latter, stir once while it is freezing.

Makes about 1¾ quarts.

Variation: FROZEN ICE-CREAM PIE

Make any kind of crumb crust (pp. 253–255). Cool. Fill with softened chocolate ice cream. Pipe whipped cream around edge, freeze.

To serve, cut into wedges and pass chocolate sauce.

PHILADELPHIA CHOCOLATE ICE CREAM

This is not as rich as the French Chocolate Ice Cream, as it con tains no egg yolks, but it is smooth and delicious.

1 quart cream, light or heavy, scalded	1 cup sugar
3 ounces chocolate (squares, melted, or envelopes)	¼ teaspoon salt
	1 tablespoon vanilla extract

1. Mix the cream, chocolate, sugar, salt, and vanilla until well blended. If necessary, heat over low heat to dissolve the sugar.

2. Freeze in an old-fashioned freezer for creamy smoothness, or in a refrigerator tray. In that case, stir once while freezing.

Makes about 1¾ quarts.

Variation: RUM PARFAIT

Whip heavy cream, adding sugar to taste and dark rum. Spoon

this and chocolate ice cream into parfait glasses in alternating layers, ending with cream on top. Decorate with a few Chocolate Curls (p. 126).

CHOCOLATE MACAROON LAYER

A lovely, luscious frozen dessert which, of course, can be made ahead of time.

1 quart heavy cream, whipped	1 teaspoon almond extract
1 cup confectioners' sugar	3 ounces chocolate, grated
1 dozen stale macaroons, crumbled	1 teaspoon vanilla extract
	½ cup chopped toasted almonds

1. Divide the whipped cream into 2 portions, or whip half at a time.

2. To one portion add ½ cup of the sugar, the macaroon crumbs, and the almond extract. Spread half of this on an 8-inch-square cake pan and put in the freezer.

3. To the other portion of the whipped cream add the grated chocolate, the vanilla, and the other ½ cup of sugar. Spread half of this over the partially frozen macaroon layer and return to the freezer.

4. When partially set, add another macaroon layer and then the rest of the chocolate cream. Be careful not to mix them. Freezing each layer as you go along helps. Sprinkle the chopped almonds on top and return to the freezer.

To serve, cut in squares and pass Rum Sauce (p. 204).

Makes 8 to 10 servings.

CHOCOLATE MACAROON MOLD

24 dried almond macaroons (2 cups crumbs)
½ cup bourbon
2 cups heavy cream

1 quart soft French Chocolate Ice Cream (pp. 165–166)

1. Put macaroon crumbs in the bottom of a gelatin mold or *bombe* mold. Pour bourbon on top and allow to soak for an hour or so.

2. Pour off any bourbon not absorbed by the crumbs and save. Remove ½ of crumbs for the top. Press the rest of the crumbs onto the inside of the mold.

3. Whip the cream and flavor it with the bourbon. Spread half on top of the crumbs. Cover this with the soft chocolate ice cream. Top with the rest of the whipped cream. Sprinkle the rest of the crumbs on top. Freeze.

Unmold and slice.

Makes 8 to 10 servings.

CHOCOLATE MINT CHARLOTTE RUSSE

A delicious dessert, perfect to end a special meal.

2 dozen ladyfingers
1 cup after-dinner mints
¾ cup milk
Few drops of red food coloring

1 cup heavy cream, whipped
2 squares semisweet chocolate, grated
Bittersweet Chocolate Sauce II (p. 199)

1. Prepare refrigerator ice-cube tray by lining it with wax paper and then with ladyfingers.

2. Melt the mints in the milk over low heat. Cool. Add food coloring to tint a delicate pink. Fold in the whipped cream and pour into another freezing tray.

3. When it has frozen to a mush, remove, stir well, and add the grated chocolate. Pour over the ladyfingers in the first tray and refreeze.

To serve, turn out so that the ladyfingers are on top. Slice. Pass Bittersweet Chocolate Sauce.

Makes 4 to 6 servings.

CINNAMON ICE CREAM

Delicious with any chocolate sauce; or try it on homemade apple pie, warm from the oven.

2 cups milk, scalded	¾ cup sugar
1-inch cinnamon stick	Red food coloring
2 tablespoons flour	1 cup heavy cream
Few grains of salt	Bittersweet Chocolate
2 tablespoons cold water	Sauce I (p. 199)
2 egg yolks	

1. Scald the milk with the cinnamon stick. Remove cinnamon.

2. Blend the flour, salt, and cold water and stir into the hot milk. Cook over low heat until thick and smooth.

3. Beat the egg yolks with the sugar. Pour the hot mixture slowly over this, stirring as you pour. Return to the stove and cook, stirring, until slightly thick. Strain and cool. Add red food coloring as desired.

4. Whip the cream and fold this into the cooled custard. Freeze. Serve with Bittersweet Chocolate Sauce.

Makes about 1½ quarts.

CINNAMON CHOCOLATE CHIP ICE CREAM

1 cup sugar	2 cups boiling water
2 tablespoons flour	1 pint heavy cream,
Pinch of salt	whipped
2 teaspoons ground cinnamon	6 ounces semisweet chocolate bits
2 tablespoons butter	

1. Mix sugar, flour, salt, cinnamon, and butter in a saucepan. Add water and cook, stirring until thick. Chill.

2. Fold cinnamon syrup into whipped cream. Add chocolate bits and freeze.

FROZEN CHOCOLATE FRUIT PUDDING

1 cup mixed glacéed fruit	2 eggs
½ cup crème de cacao	1 cup sugar
2 ounces chocolate (squares, melted, or envelopes)	Few grains of salt
	1 cup heavy cream
2½ cups hot milk	

1. Combine the fruit and the liqueur and let stand overnight.

2. Stir chocolate and milk in the top of a double boiler over boiling water until blended.

3. Beat eggs thoroughly and add the sugar and salt. Mix well. Pour chocolate-milk mixture in slowly, beating as you pour. Cook, stirring, until the custard coats the spoon. Cool.

4. Whip the cream and fold it and the fruit into the chocolate mixture. Pour into a 2-quart melon mold and freeze.

Makes about 2 quarts.

FROZEN CHOCOLATE MOUSSE

¼ cup sugar	3 egg yolks
½ cup orange juice	1 cup heavy cream, whipped
1 cup semisweet chocolate bits	¼ cup Grand Marnier

1. Combine sugar, juice, and chocolate bits, and simmer until the chocolate is melted and all is blended. Cool slightly.

2. Beat egg yolks and add the chocolate mixture slowly, beating as you add. Fold in the whipped cream and the liqueur. Spread in a refrigerator tray, cover with foil, and freeze until firm.

Makes 6 to 8 servings.

Note: See Bittersweet Chocolate Mousse (p. 149).

FROZEN STRAWBERRY LAYER

    1 cup water
    ¾ cup sugar
    10 egg yolks
    1 cup hazelnuts, ground
      fine or put through a
      blender
    2 ounces chocolate
      (squares, melted and
      cooled, or envelopes)
    4 tablespoons Curaçao
    2 cups heavy cream,
      whipped
    1 package (10 ounces)
      frozen strawberries,
      thawed
    Sweet chocolate, grated

1. Make a syrup of the water and sugar. Cool.

2. Beat the egg yolks until they are thick and light in color. Add the syrup slowly and beat well. Then add the nuts, chocolate, and Curaçao. Mix well. Fold in the whipped cream. Spread half of the cream mixture in a 3-quart mold. Put the thawed strawberries through a blender and spread over the top. Spread the rest of the chocolate mixture over the top of this layer. Freeze.

To serve, slice. Serve with additional whipped cream, or unmold and top with grated sweet chocolate.

Makes 10 to 12 servings.

FROZEN RASPBERRY SQUARES

This is a beautiful and unusual dessert.

1 cup chocolate wafer crumbs (12 to 15 cookies)
3 tablespoons melted butter
1 teaspoon vanilla extract
¼ cup pistachios, put through a blender

1½ quarts soft pistachio ice cream
1 jar (8 ounces) seedless raspberry jam
Chocolate Sauce (pp. 199–205)

1. Line 2 ice-cube trays with wax paper or foil.

2. Mix the crumbs, butter, vanilla, and nuts thoroughly. Spread half of the crumbs on the bottom of the trays. Spread the ice cream on this. Top with a layer of raspberry jam. Spread the rest of the crumbs on top. Freeze in the freezer compartment of a refrigerator or in a freezer.

To serve, cut into squares and pass your favorite Chocolate Sauce.

Makes 10 to 12 servings.

GRASSHOPPER PARFAIT

Try this for a light dessert.

1 jigger (3 tablespoons) crème de cacao
1 jigger (3 tablespoons) crème de menthe

2 scoops vanilla ice cream
Chocolate shot

Put the liqueurs and 1 scoop of ice cream in an electric blender and blend briefly. Spoon into a tall chilled glass. Add another scoop of ice cream, and top with chocolate shot.

Makes 1 serving.

LIQUEUR SHERBET

½ cup crème de cacao   1 quart soft orange ice

Blend both ingredients and return to freezer until firm.
Serve with chocolate cookies.
Makes 6 servings.

MERINGUE SHELLS WITH ICE CREAM FILLING

Use these as a base for building up a chocolate dessert. They keep for a few days if wrapped lightly in wax paper.

2 egg whites   Pinch of salt
1 teaspoon vanilla extract   ½ cup granulated sugar
½ teaspoon cream of tartar   Sifted confectioners' sugar

1. Place unglazed paper on a cooky sheet.

2. Beat egg whites until frothy. Add, while continuing to beat, the vanilla, cream of tartar, and salt. Add the granulated sugar very slowly while you beat. Beat until stiff peaks are formed.

3. Spoon the meringue on the paper in circles, keeping them 2 inches apart. Make a hollow in the center of each one to hold the ice cream. Sprinkle each with a little confectioners' sugar.

4. Bake in a 250° F. oven for about 1 hour, or until the meringues feel dry when touched lightly. Remove from paper with a spatula. Return to oven for 5 minutes to dry completely. Cool on a rack.

To serve, fill with your favorite ice cream and pour Rich Chocolate Sauce (pp. 201–202) on top. Sprinkle with pistachio nuts.

GELATIN DESSERTS

GELATIN DESSERTS often team well with chocolate sauce.

To unmold a gelatin dessert: Rinse the mold in cold water before filling it with the gelatin. When the gelatin is set, dip the mold quickly into hot water and shake to loosen the dessert. It may be necessary to dip it again. Just the right amount of heat will loosen it without melting the gelatin. Place a serving plate over the top of the mold, and turn upside down. Another shake will drop the mold on the plate. If the plate is moistened first, you can move the dessert slightly in case it has been turned out a little off center, as often happens.

BANANA MOLD WITH CHOCOLATE SAUCE

2½ tablespoons unflavored gelatin
¼ cup orange juice
2 cups boiling water
½ cup sugar
2 tablespoons lemon juice

2 teaspoons grated lemon rind
Few grains of salt
4 ripe bananas, mashed
1 tablespoon Cointreau
Chocolate Sauce with Cointreau (p. 201)

1. Rinse a 1-quart mold with cold water.

2. Soak the gelatin in the orange juice. When soft, add the boiling water and stir to dissolve. Stir in the sugar, lemon juice and rind, and salt. Put in refrigerator until partially set.

3. When the mixture begins to thicken, stir in the bananas and the Cointreau. Pour into the rinsed mold and return to the refrigerator.

To serve, unmold on a serving plate and pass cold Chocolate Sauce with Cointreau.

Makes 6 servings.

CHOCOLATE ANGEL REFRIGERATOR DESSERT

1 8-inch angel-food cake
2 tablespoons unflavored gelatin
¼ cup cold water
4 ounces chocolate (squares, cut up, or envelopes)

1½ cups hot water
6 eggs, separated
⅔ cup sugar
2 cups heavy cream
1 teaspoon vanilla extract
4 ounces semisweet chocolate, grated

1. Cut angel-food cake into squares, about 1-inch size. Put them in a bowl.

2. Soak the gelatin in the cold water.

3. Mix the chocolate and hot water. Stir over low heat until smooth. Stir in the gelatin. Cool.

4. Beat egg yolks until thick and light. Beat in the chocolate mixture slowly.

5. Beat egg whites until they are fairly stiff, then add the sugar gradually. Beat until peaks are formed. Fold into the chocolate mixture. Spoon the chocolate meringue on top of the cake cubes, and fold all together gently. Pour into a 10-inch angel-cake pan which has been rinsed in cold water. Refrigerate to set. Unmold on a serving plate.

6. Whip the cream, add the vanilla and grated chocolate. Spoon half of it into the center of the unmolded dessert. Pass the rest in a bowl.

Makes 8 to 10 servings.

CHOCOLATE BAVARIAN CREAM

1½ teaspoons unflavored gelatin	½ cup sugar
2 tablespoons cold water	2 eggs, separated
1 cup semisweet chocolate bits	3 tablespoons dark rum
	Pinch of salt
	½ cup heavy cream

1. Soak the gelatin in the water in the top of a double boiler. Add the chocolate bits and ¼ cup of the sugar. Place over hot water and heat, stirring, until the chocolate is melted and the whole is blended.

2. Beat the egg yolks and rum together, and pour the hot mixture slowly into this, stirring as you pour.

3. Beat the egg whites until they are foamy throughout. Add the salt, then the remaining ¼ cup sugar gradually, continuing to beat until the mixture stands in peaks. Fold this into the chocolate mixture.

4. Whip the cream and fold it in. Pour all into a 1-quart mold that has been rinsed with cold water. Refrigerate until set.

To serve, turn out on a serving plate and serve with whipped cream flavored with additional rum.

Makes 4 servings.

CHOCOLATE CHARLOTTE RUSSE

A wonderful dessert for special occasions.

18 ladyfingers
2 tablespoons unflavored
   gelatin
½ cup cold water
2 cups milk
2 ounces chocolate
   (squares, melted,
   or envelopes)

6 egg yolks
1 cup sugar
2 cups heavy cream,
   whipped
2 teaspoons vanilla extract

1. Line a 10-inch springform pan with wax paper and then with the ladyfingers.

2. Soak the gelatin in the cold water to soften.

3. Blend the milk and the chocolate over hot water.

4. Beat the yolks until thick and lemon-colored, then beat in the sugar. Pour in the hot chocolate mixture very slowly, beating as you pour. Cook over hot water until thick and smooth. Add the softened gelatin and stir to dissolve. Place in the refrigerator. When partially set and thick and syrupy, fold in the whipped cream and the vanilla. Return to refrigerator.

To serve, unmold on a serving tray. Cut into slices. Pass a bowl of additional whipped cream, topped with grated semisweet chocolate.

Makes 8 to 10 servings.

CHOCOLATE CRÈME

This rich pudding may be served topped with whipped cream, or it may be used as a pie filling or to fill a Schaumtorte (pp. 90–91).

3 ounces chocolate (squares, cut up, or envelopes)
¾ cup rich milk or half-and-half
1 tablespoon unflavored gelatin

¼ cup cold water
⅓ cup plus ½ cup sugar
2 tablespoons cornstarch
Pinch of salt
3 eggs, separated
2 tablespoons rum
1 cup heavy cream, whipped

1. Soften the gelatin in the cold water.

2. Combine chocolate and milk. Simmer, stirring, until the chocolate is melted and the mixture blended.

3. Mix ⅓ cup sugar, the cornstarch, salt, and the softened gelatin. Add the hot chocolate mixture, and stir to dissolve gelatin.

4. Beat egg yolks until light and creamy. Add the hot mixture slowly, beating as you pour. Set aside to cool slightly.

5. Beat egg whites until foamy throughout. Add the ½ cup sugar gradually and continue beating until stiff peaks are formed. Fold in the chocolate mixture slowly. Add the rum and blend.

6. Whip the cream and fold this in also. Spoon into a serving bowl or individual dishes, or into a pie shell. Top this with whipped cream if you like.

Makes 6 servings.

CHOCOLATE CRÈME AU RHUM

1 tablespoon unflavored gelatin
¼ cup cold water
1 pound dark sweet chocolate (such as German's)

½ cup water
10 eggs, separated
¼ cup dark rum
Whipped cream
Strawberries and leaves (optional)

1. Rinse a 1-quart melon mold with cold water.

2. Soak the gelatin in the ¼ cup cold water.

3. Combine the chocolate and the ½ cup water and stir over low heat until well blended. Add the gelatin and stir to dissolve.

4. Beat the egg yolks until light and thick. Add the rum. Pour in the chocolate mixture very slowly, beating as you pour.

5. Beat the egg whites until stiff and fold gently into the first mixture. Pour into the mold and refrigerate to set.

To serve, unmold on a serving platter and pipe whipped cream around the base. Decorate with fresh strawberries and strawberry leaves, if available.

Makes 6 servings.

CHOCOLATE MACAROON CREAM

12 macaroons, crumbled	1 ounce chocolate
½ cup sherry	(square, melted,
2 tablespoons unflavored	or envelope)
gelatin	4 eggs, separated
¼ cup water	½ cup heavy cream,
2 cups hot milk	whipped
	1 teaspoon almond extract

1. Rinse a 1-quart mold with cold water.

2. Soak the macaroons in the sherry.

3. Combine the gelatin and the water and set aside.

4. Stir the milk and chocolate over low heat to blend. Pour over the gelatin. Stir to dissolve the gelatin.

5. Beat the egg yolks until thick and lemon-colored. Slowly pour the chocolate mixture over these, beating as you pour. Stir in the macaroons and sherry.

6. Beat egg whites until they form soft peaks and gently fold them into the chocolate mixture. Pour into the prepared mold. Refrigerate until set.

To serve, unmold onto a serving dish. Surround the pudding with the whipped cream flavored with almond extract.

Makes 6 to 8 servings.

CHOCOLATE MINT DREAM WHIP

1 cup semisweet chocolate bits
1 cup light cream
1 tablespoon unflavored gelatin
¼ cup cold water
4 eggs

½ cup sugar
1 cup heavy cream, whipped
2 teaspoons vanilla extract
½ teaspoon peppermint extract

1. Stir the chocolate and the light cream in the top of a double boiler over hot water until the chocolate is melted and the two blended.

2. Soak the gelatin in the cold water.

3. Beat the eggs well and add the sugar gradually, continuing to beat until the mixture is thick and creamy. Stir the chocolate mixture slowly into this, beating as you add. Pour back into the top of the double boiler and cook over simmering water for about 5 minutes, stirring. Add the gelatin and stir to dissolve. Remove from the heat and cool. Allow to partially set.

4. When the pudding has begun to thicken, fold in the whipped cream and the flavorings. Pour into a 1½-quart mold or serving bowl and place in the refrigerator to set.

Makes 6 to 8 servings.

CHOCOLATE ORANGE BAVARIAN SPONGE

2 tablespoons unflavored
gelatin
½ cup orange juice
½ cup hot water
4 ounces chocolate
(squares, cut up,
or envelopes)
1 cup sugar
Pinch of salt

2 eggs, separated
2 cups milk
1 teaspoon vanilla extract
2 teaspoons grated orange
rind
1 cup heavy cream,
whipped
2 tablespoons Grand
Marnier

1. Rinse a 2-quart mold with cold water.

2. Soak the gelatin in the orange juice.

3. Combine the hot water, chocolate, half of the sugar, and the salt in a saucepan. Cook and stir until blended. Add gelatin and stir to dissolve. Cool slightly.

4. Beat the egg yolks well. Stir in the chocolate mixture slowly, then add the milk and the vanilla. Add the orange rind. Put in the refrigerator to set partially.

5. Beat the egg whites until stiff and beat in the rest of the sugar slowly. When the meringue stands in soft peaks, fold it into the partially set gelatin. Then fold in the whipped cream and the liqueur. Pour the pudding into the mold. Return to the refrigerator to set.

To serve, unmold onto a serving tray and surround with more whipped cream and orange sections.

A sauce of orange marmalade, orange juice, and Grand Marnier is good with this.

Makes 8 to 10 servings.

CHOCOLATE PECAN MOLD

This will remind you of a Torte, though it is made with gelatin. It makes a perfect hot-weather party dessert and, of course, can be made the day before, which is always a blessing.

½ cup chocolate-wafer crumbs (10 or 15 wafers)

½ cup pecans, finely chopped or put through a blender

1 tablespoon unflavored gelatin

¼ cup cold water

6 ounces semisweet chocolate bits

¾ cup sugar

Pinch of salt

½ cup milk

3 eggs, separated

1 cup heavy cream, whipped

1 teaspoon vanilla extract

1. **Rinse a 10-inch springform pan with cold water and line it with wax paper. Mix the crumbs and nuts and press half of them in the bottom of the pan.**

2. **Soak gelatin in the cold water.**

3. **Put the chocolate, ½ cup of the sugar, the salt, and milk in the top of a double boiler. Cook over simmering water, stirring, until the mixture is thick and hot.**

4. **Beat the egg yolks until thick and lemon-colored. Stir in the hot chocolate mixture slowly, beating as you add, and return all to the double boiler over hot water until thick. Add the soaked gelatin and stir until dissolved. Chill until the mixture begins to set.**

5. **Beat egg whites until stiff but not dry. Beat in the remaining ¼ cup sugar gradually, and then fold this into the thickened gelatin mixture. Fold in the cream and vanilla also. Spoon the pudding into the pan on top of the crumbs and nuts. Sprinkle the rest of them on top of the pudding. Refrigerate to set.**

To serve, unmold and pass additional whipped cream.

Makes 8 to 10 servings.

COFFEE CHOCOLATE JELLY

This is a delicious light dessert.

1 tablespoon unflavored
gelatin
½ cup cold water
½ cup sugar
⅓ cup cocoa

1 tablespoon instant coffee powder
Pinch of salt
1½ cups hot water
1 teaspoon vanilla extract
Whipped cream

1. Rinse a 1-quart mold with cold water.

2. Put gelatin in the ½ cup cold water.

3. Mix sugar, cocoa, coffee powder, salt, and hot water in a saucepan. Bring to a boil and cook, stirring, for a minute or two. Add gelatin and stir until dissolved. Add the vanilla. Pour into the prepared mold and place in the refrigerator to set.

To serve, unmold and pipe whipped cream around the edge. Pass more whipped cream.

Makes 4 servings.

COFFEE CHOCOLATE MOLD

This is similar to the preceeding dessert, but it is made with chocolate syrup and has the cream folded in rather than served on top.

1 tablespoon unflavored
gelatin
¼ cup cold water
1 cup Chocolate Syrup (p. 205)

2 teaspoons instant coffee
powder
¼ cup water
1 cup heavy cream

1. Rinse a 1-quart mold with cold water.

2. Soak the gelatin in the ¼ cup cold water.

3. Stir the syrup, coffee powder, and ¼ cup water over low heat until blended. Add the gelatin, stirring until dissolved. Set in the refrigerator to thicken slightly.

4. Whip the cream and fold it into the partially set gelatin mixture. Pour into the prepared mold, and refrigerate until completely set.

To serve, unmold on a serving plate and pass additional whipped cream, if desired.

Makes 4 to 6 servings.

COFFEE CHOCOLATE SPONGE

Here is another pudding with the popular coffee-chocolate combination.

1 tablespoon unflavored gelatin	1 cup sugar
¼ cup cold water	½ cup milk
2 ounces chocolate (squares, cut up, or envelopes)	4 eggs, separated
	1 teaspoon vanilla extract
	Pinch of salt
1½ cups hot water	Whipped cream
	Candied violets

1. Rinse a 2-quart mold with cold water.

2. Soak the gelatin in the ¼ cup cold water.

3. Combine the chocolate, hot water, and ½ cup of the sugar in a saucepan. Cook over low heat, stirring, until the chocolate is melted and the mixture is smooth. Add the soaked gelatin and stir to dissolve. Add the milk.

4. Beat the egg yolks well. Beat in the remaining ½ cup of sugar and the vanilla. Pour the chocolate mixture over the yolks slowly, beating as you pour. Place in refrigerator to partially set.

5. Whip the egg whites and salt until stiff. Fold into the partially set gelatin mixture. Pour into the mold and return to the refrigerator.

To serve, unmold on a serving dish. Surround with whipped cream, decorated with chocolate leaves.

Makes 6 to 8 servings.

CRÈME DE CACAO SPONGE

3 eggs, separated
1½ cups milk
½ cup cocoa
½ cup sugar
1 tablespoon unflavored gelatin

2 teaspoons vanilla extract
Pinch of salt
2 tablespoons crème de cacao
Chocolate Curls (p. 126)

1. Rinse a 1-quart mold with cold water.

2. Beat the egg yolks well and add the milk.

3. Mix the cocoa, ¼ cup of the sugar, and the gelatin. Beat into the egg-yolk and milk mixture and pour all into the top of a double boiler. Heat over boiling water, stirring until the gelatin is dissolved. Remove from the heat. Add the vanilla, salt, and crème de cacao. Chill until partially set.

4. Whip the egg whites until stiff and add the remaining ¼ cup sugar slowly. When soft peaks are formed, fold this into the gelatin, which should be thick but not set. Pour into prepared mold and refrigerate.

To serve, unmold on a serving plate, surround with whipped cream, and decorate with Chocolate Curls.

Makes 6 to 8 servings.

CHOCOLATE SOUFFLÉ

2 tablespoons unflavored gelatin
2 cups milk
1 cup sugar
¼ teaspoon salt
4 eggs, separated

12 ounces (2 cups) semi-sweet chocolate bits
2 teaspoons vanilla extract
2 cups heavy cream, whipped.

1. Soak gelatin in ½ cup of the milk.

2. Put this, with the rest of the milk, ½ cup of the sugar, the salt and the egg yolks, in a saucepan. Stir to mix. Add chocolate. Place over low heat, stirring constantly, until the gelatin is dissolved and the chocolate melted. Cool.

3. Add the vanilla, and beat with a rotary beater until the chocolate is blended. Place in the refrigerator to partially set.

4. Beat the egg whites until stiff but not dry. Beat in the remaining ½ cup sugar gradually. When this meringue is very stiff, fold it into the chocolate mixture. Fold in the whipped cream. Pour into a 2-quart soufflé dish, on which you have taped a 3-inch collar of foil. Return to the refrigerator to set.

To serve, remove the collar and decorate with additional whipped cream, or pass it in a sauce boat.

Makes 12 servings.

HONEY ALMOND BAVARIAN CREAM

2 tablespoons unflavored gelatin	6 tablespoons sugar
¼ cup cold water	½ cup water
2 ounces unsweetened chocolate (squares, cut up, or envelopes)	3 egg whites
	1½ cups heavy cream
	1 teaspoon almond extract
1 cup honey	1 cup chopped toasted almonds
	Chocolate Curls (p. 126)

1. Rinse a 1½-quart mold with cold water.

2. Soak the gelatin in the ¼ cup cold water.

3. Mix the chocolate, honey, sugar, and ½ cup of water in a saucepan, and cook to the soft-ball stage, which is 238° F. on a candy thermometer. Stir in the gelatin to dissolve.

4. Beat the egg whites until stiff and very slowly pour the chocolate syrup over them, beating as you pour. Cool slightly.

5. Whip the cream stiff, add the almond extract, and fold this into the chocolate and gelatin mixture. Fold in ¾ cup of the almonds. Pour into the prepared mold, and put in refrigerator to set.

To serve, unmold on a serving platter and surround with additional whipped cream. Garnish with the rest of the almonds and Chocolate Curls.

Makes 8 to 10 servings.

PEPPERMINT SPONGE WITH CHOCOLATE SAUCE

1 tablespoon unflavored gelatin	Few drops of green food coloring
¼ cup cold water	2 cups heavy cream
½ cup light cream	Whipped cream
½ cup sugar	Candied mint leaves
½ teaspoon peppermint extract	Bittersweet Chocolate Sauce (p. 199)

1. Rinse a 1-quart mold with cold water.

2. Soak the gelatin in the ¼ cup cold water.

3. Heat the light cream—do not boil—and pour it over the softened gelatin. Stir to dissolve thoroughly. Add the sugar, peppermint, and green coloring. Put in the refrigerator to set partially.

4. Whip half of the cream stiff and fold into the gelatin which has just begun to thicken. Pour into the prepared mold, and return to the refrigerator.

To serve, unmold and surround with the remaining cream, whipped. Garnish with candied mint leaves. Pass Bittersweet Chocolate Sauce.

Makes 4 to 6 servings.

REFRIGERATOR DESSERTS

CHOCOLATE RUM REFRIGERATOR DESSERT

This creamy rich dessert is of Italian origin.

1 cup unsalted butter	Pinch of salt
¼ cup sugar	1½ cups almonds
6 ounces chocolate	¼ cup dark rum
(squares, melted and	½ package vanilla wafers
cooled, or envelopes)	(about 12)
2 eggs, separated	Whipped cream

1. Oil a loaf pan (9 x 5 x 3 inches) lightly with vegetable oil.

2. Cream the butter with the sugar, beating until it is light and fluffy. Stir in the cooled chocolate. Beat in the egg yolks, one at a time, and the salt.

3. Grind the almonds, or put them through your blender. Add these.

4. Beat the egg whites until stiff but not dry. Fold these into the pudding. Add the rum, and the wafers, broken into rather large pieces; discard the crumbs. Spoon the mixture into the prepared pan, pressing down well. Chill overnight.

To serve, unmold on a serving platter and surround with whipped cream flavored with a little rum.

Makes 8 servings.

GÂTEAU ÉLÉGANT

This is a beautiful dessert, delectably rich.

1 cup almonds	2½ cups sugar
1 cup hazelnuts	

1. Start by making glacéed nuts as follows:

Place the nuts and the sugar in a heavy skillet and stir over medium heat until the sugar has become liquid and golden. Turn onto a baking sheet to cool.

2. Break up the candy and put it through a blender until very fine.

Now make the dessert itself:

7 egg yolks
6 tablespoons plus ½ cup confectioners' sugar
4 cups milk
2 tablespoons sherry
¾ pound unsalted butter
2 ounces chocolate (squares, melted and cooled, or envelopes)

1 tablespoon vanilla extract
1½ dozen chocolate wafers (enough to line 2 loaf pans)
1 cup heavy cream, whipped
Crystallized mint leaves

1. Beat the egg yolks and the 6 tablespoons sugar until very thick. Put in the top of a double boiler with the milk and cook over simmering water, stirring, until the custard coats the spoon. Cool.

2. Add the sherry and set aside.

3. Cream the butter and the ½ cup sugar until light and fluffy. Add 6 tablespoons of the cold custard and the cooled chocolate. Stir in the glacéed nuts and the vanilla.

4. Line two loaf pans (9 x 5 x 3 inches) with the chocolate wafers, and spoon the nut mixture on top. Cover with wax paper and chill.

To serve, turn out and pipe whipped cream around the edge of the pudding.

Decorate with the mint leaves.

Pass the cold custard in a sauceboat.

Makes 12 to 18 servings.

MEXICAN PECAN CREAM

4 slices of stale spongecake
2 cups heavy cream
1 cup confectioners' sugar
1 teaspoon instant coffee powder
Pinch of salt
1 teaspoon vanilla extract

4 egg yolks
2 ounces chocolate (squares, melted and cooled, or envelopes)
½ cup chopped pecans

1. Arrange the cake slices in the bottom of a serving dish.

2. Whip the cream, but stop just short of making it stiff.

3. Stir the sugar, coffee powder, salt, vanilla, and egg yolks into the chocolate. Blend well. Fold this into the cream. Spread the cream mixture on the cake slices, sprinkle the nuts on top, and chill well before serving.

Makes 6 to 8 servings.

MOCHA LIQUEUR REFRIGERATOR CAKE

A dessert with a wonderful flavor, and easy to put together.

1 cup heavy cream
1 tablespoon confectioners' sugar
1 teaspoon unflavored gelatin

2 tablespoons Kahlua or any coffee liqueur
1 package (8 ounces) thin chocolate wafers

1. Whip the cream and fold in the sugar, gelatin, and liqueur.

2. Spread the chocolate wafers with the cream, using the whole package of wafers and half of the cream. Stand the wafers on end as you put them together. Cover the outside of the roll with the rest of the cream. Refrigerate it for several hours.

To serve, slice diagonally. Pass chocolate sauce.

Makes 4 to 6 servings.

PORCUPINE CAKE

In spite of its odd name, you will find this refrigerator dessert creamy and rich, a real delight.

2 dozen ladyfingers	Few grains of salt
Sherry	½ cup sugar
6 ounces chocolate (squares, melted, or envelopes)	1 cup unsalted butter
	1 tablespoon vanilla extract
3 tablespoons strong coffee	Toasted slivered almonds
4 egg yolks	

1. Line a 1-quart mold with wax paper. A melon mold will carry out the porcupine idea, but any other shape will serve. Cover the bottom with some of the ladyfingers dipped briefly into the sherry.

2. Blend the chocolate and coffee.

3. Beat the egg yolks and add the salt. Add the sugar gradually. Beat until thick and creamy. Add the chocolate and stir over hot water until the mixture is thick and smooth. Remove from the heat and add the butter, a small amount at a time, stirring in well as you add. Stir in the vanilla. Cool.

4. Spoon a layer of the chocolate over the ladyfingers, add another layer of ladyfingers dipped into sherry, then a layer of chocolate, etc., saving some of the chocolate for the outside. Refrigerate overnight.

To serve, unmold on a serving tray. Spread the outside with the remaining chocolate cream, and stud the cake with almonds.

Makes 6 to 8 servings

SAUCES AND SYRUPS

*S*ome are chocolate, some merely bring out the chocolate flavor of the dessert they are used with—but all are delicious.

APRICOT RUM SAUCE

This is a delicious but very simple rum sauce for chocolate ice cream.

1 cup apricot jam   ½ cup dark rum

Heat the jam in the top of a double boiler. Add the rum and blend.

You may serve it as it is, or you may ignite it and pour it flaming over the ice cream.

Makes about 1½ cups.

BITTERSWEET CHOCOLATE SAUCE I

5 ounces chocolate (squares, cut up, or envelopes)
¾ cup milk
1 cup sugar
Pinch of salt
¼ cup butter
1 tablespoon vanilla extract
2 tablespoons sherry

Put the chocolate, milk, sugar, salt, and butter in the top of a double boiler. Cook and stir over simmering water until the ingredients are blended and the sauce is thick and smooth. Remove from the heat. Stir in the butter. Cool. Add the vanilla and the sherry. Serve warm or cold.

Makes about 2½ cups.

BITTERSWEET CHOCOLATE SAUCE II

8 ounces chocolate (squares, cut up, or envelopes)
2 cups sugar
1 small can (5½ ounces) evaporated milk, undiluted
¼ cup butter
1 tablespoon vanilla extract

1. Put chocolate, sugar, and evaporated milk in the top of a double boiler. Heat over simmering water, stirring, until well blended. Add the butter. Cool. Add the vanilla.

2. This sauce is very thick. Store it in a jar in the refrigerator, and thin it with hot water to the desired consistency, as you use it.

Makes about 2 cups of thick sauce—more when diluted as desired.

BLENDER FUDGE SAUCE

½ cup heavy cream
1 cup semisweet chocolate bits

Few grains of salt
1 tablespoon vanilla extract

Heat the cream over low heat; do not boil. Put in an electric blender and add the chocolate and salt. Blend for 1 minute. Add the vanilla and blend on high speed for 5 or 6 seconds.

Makes about 1½ cups.

BRANDY HAZELNUT SAUCE

6 tablespoons soft butter
⅔ cup confectioners' sugar
3 egg yolks
1 cup heavy cream

2 tablespoons brandy
½ cup hazelnuts, chopped fine or put through an electric blender

1. Cream the butter and sugar. Beat in the egg yolks and pour into the top of a double boiler. Add the cream and cook over simmering water until thick and smooth. Remove from the heat and add the brandy and nuts. Blend. Serve warm over chocolate ice cream.

Makes about 2 cups.

BROWN-SUGAR SHERRY SAUCE

1½ cups firmly packed brown sugar
1 cup milk

Pinch of salt
1 tablespoon butter
1 tablespoon sherry

Boil the sugar, milk, and salt until the mixture forms a very soft ball in water, 238° F. on a candy thermometer. Remove from the heat and add the butter and sherry. Stir to blend. Serve cold or warm. This is especially good with chocolate ice cream.

Makes about 2½ cups.

CHOCOLATE SAUCE WITH COINTREAU

3 ounces chocolate
(squares, cut up, or
envelopes)
¾ cup sugar

1 cup heavy cream
Few grains of salt
2 tablespoons Cointreau

Mix everything together except the Cointreau. Cook over low heat, stirring, until the mixture is smooth and thick. Remove from the heat. Cool. Add the Cointreau.

Makes about 2 cups.

CINNAMON SAUCE

1 cup sugar
2 tablespoons flour
Few grains of salt
2 teaspoons ground cinna-
mon

2 cups boiling water
2 tablespoons butter
Juice of ½ lemon

Mix the sugar, flour, salt, and cinnamon in a saucepan. Stir in the boiling water and cook until the sauce is thick and smooth. Add the butter and lemon juice.

Serve warm or cold. This is delicious on any kind of chocolate ice cream, as well as on Ginger Chocolate Cake (pp. 45–46) or Mocha Raisin Cake (pp. 50–51).

Makes about 2½ cups.

RICH CHOCOLATE SAUCE

½ cup butter
2 ounces unsweetened
chocolate (squares,
cut up, or
envelopes)
½ cup cocoa

1 small can (5½ ounces)
evaporated milk, undi-
luted
Few grains of salt
1 teaspoon vanilla extract
½ cup sherry

Put all the ingredients except the vanilla and the sherry in a saucepan. Cook over low heat, stirring, until the chocolate is melted and all is blended. When the sauce almost comes to a boil, remove from the heat and cool. Add the vanilla and sherry, and stir to mix.

Makes about 2 cups.

HONEY BUTTER

¼ cup butter
¼ cup honey

2 tablespoons heavy cream

Cream the butter, beat the honey in slowly, and then the cream. Delicious on ice cream, waffles, cake, or pudding. Try this on chocolate pancakes, too.

Makes about ½ cup.

HONEY CHOCOLATE SAUCE

1 cup semisweet chocolate bits
½ cup honey

¾ cup cream
1 teaspoon cornstarch

1. Melt the chocolate bits in the honey over low heat.

2. Mix the cream and cornstarch. Stir this into the chocolate-honey mixture. Simmer until the sauce is thick and smooth.

Makes about 2¼ cups.

ORANGE CHOCOLATE SAUCE

8 ounces semisweet chocolate
¼ cup Curaçao
¼ cup water

¼ cup confectioners' sugar
2 tablespoons grated orange rind

Melt the chocolate in the top of a double boiler over simmering water. Add the other ingredients and stir over direct heat until the sauce is thick and smooth.

Makes about 2 cups.

ORANGE SAUCE

Try this on Cocoa Angel Food (pp. 59–60) or Chocolate Soufflé (p. 154).

¾ cup sugar	2 oranges, juice and
1½ tablespoons corn-	grated rind
starch	3 egg yolks
Pinch of salt	1 cup heavy cream

1. Mix the sugar, cornstarch, and salt in the top of a double boiler. Stir in the orange juice and cook over hot water until the sauce is thick.

2. Beat the egg yolks. Add the orange rind. Pour the hot mixture over these slowly, beating as you pour. Return to the heat and cook for a few minutes more. Cool.

3. Whip the cream and fold the two together.

Makes about 3 cups.

RICH CHOCOLATE CUSTARD SAUCE

2 cups rich milk	⅔ cup sugar
4 ounces chocolate	1 teaspoon cornstarch
(squares, melted,	½ cup heavy cream,
or envelopes)	whipped
4 egg yolks	1 teaspoon vanilla extract
	1 tablespoon cognac

1. Place the milk and the chocolate in the top of a double boiler. Heat over hot water until well blended.

2. Beat egg yolks until creamy, then add the sugar mixed with the cornstarch, and beat again. Beat in the hot chocolate mixture, adding it slowly. Continue to cook over hot water until the custard thickens slightly. Cool, stirring occasionally to prevent a crust from forming. Fold in the whipped cream, vanilla, and cognac.

Serve cold with any pudding or for any special dessert.

Makes about 3½ cups.

RUM SAUCE

1 cup sugar	2 tablespoons butter
2 tablespoons cornstarch	2 tablespoons lemon juice
Pinch of salt	4 tablespoons dark rum
2 cups boiling water	

Mix the sugar, cornstarch, and salt together. Pour the boiling water over slowly and cook, stirring, until the sauce comes to a boil. Continue to cook for 5 or 6 minutes. Stir in the butter, lemon juice, and rum.

Serve hot or cold over chocolate pudding or ice cream. Good on mince pie, too.

Makes about 3½ cups.

THIN CHOCOLATE SAUCE

If you like a thin, not-too-rich sauce, this will be perfect.

1 cup sugar	Few grains of salt
½ cup water	1 teaspoon vanilla extract
2 ounces chocolate (squares, melted, or envelopes)	

Make a syrup of the sugar and water. Stir in the chocolate until well blended. Add the salt and vanilla. Serve hot or cold.

Makes about 1½ cups.

CHOCOLATE SYRUP

A dark, delicious syrup for beverages or desserts.

5 ounces chocolate
(squares or
envelopes)
1⅓ cups hot water

1 cup sugar
Pinch of salt
1 teaspoon vanilla extract

Simmer chocolate and water until well blended. Add sugar and salt. Simmer for 5 minutes, stirring while it cooks. Cool. Add vanilla.

Try pouring this over a cake warm from the oven.

Makes 2 cups.

CINNAMON SYRUP

Use this to serve on Chocolate Spice Cake (p. 38). Try it also over chocolate ice cream.

4 cups apple juice
1 cup light corn syrup

½ cup red cinnamon drops
1 cinnamon stick (2
inches)

Mix all together and simmer until reduced to about 2½ cups. Store in the refrigerator until needed.

COCOA SYRUP

Use this syrup as a base for cocoa beverages or for dessert toppings.

1 cup cocoa
1¼ cups sugar
Pinch of salt

1¼ cups water
1 teaspoon vanilla extract

Mix together all ingredients except the vanilla. Stir over low heat until the syrup comes to a boil. Simmer for 5 minutes, stirring while it cooks. Cool. Add vanilla.

Makes 3½ cups.

COFFEE SYRUP

This is delicious spread on any kind of a cake, hot or cold. It may be topped with whipped cream or frosting.

1 cup sugar	⅔ cup water
1 teaspoon instant coffee powder	1 tablespoon dark rum

Mix the sugar, coffee powder, and water in a saucepan. Bring to a boil and boil for 1 minute. Cool slightly. Add rum.

Makes 1⅔ cups.

SPICED RUM SYRUP

We like this poured over Chocolate Spice Cake (p. 38), or a cake such as Chocolate Hazelnut Layer Cake (pp. 34–35), made with rum in the recipe instead of the bourbon.

1 cup sugar	1-inch cinnamon stick
1¼ cups water	1 lemon slice
3 whole cloves	¼ cup light rum
½ teaspoon grated nutmeg	

Mix the sugar, water, cloves, nutmeg, cinnamon stick, and lemon. Simmer for 5 minutes over low heat. Remove the cinnamon stick and cloves. Cool. Add the rum.

Makes 2½ cups.

COOKIES

P TIPS FOR STORING COOKIES

ERSONALLY, I see no reason for filling my freezer with baked cookies except just before Christmas time, when I wish to have many varieties ready to pack in attractive boxes to give as gifts.

Some Christmas cookies, such as Springerle, Pfeffernüsse, and Lebkuchen, need a few weeks to ripen, so I start making them around Thanksgiving and store them in airtight boxes on my pantry shelf.

Then come the other varieties rich in butter and nuts, which keep very well, but I pack them away in the freezer until Christmas so that when friends receive them, they are assured of the keeping qualities of the gift.

So ordinarily I keep only a box or two of baked cookies in the freezer for emergencies, and have some frozen cooky dough on hand to bake so that I can serve fresh and fragrant cookies when I need them.

Baked cookies will keep for about 8 months, unbaked cookies for 6 months in the freezer.

Rolled Cookies. Put unbaked cookies on buttered cooky sheets and freeze them. Stack them with a double layer of freezer paper between the layers. Wrap, and label them with the date, the name of the variety, the number of cookies, and baking directions. You may bake these without defrosting.

Refrigerator Cookies. Shape the dough in a roll and wrap in freezer paper. Label with the date, name of cooky, and baking directions. To bake, slice them frozen and bake without thawing.

Drop Cookies. Follow the directions for rolled cookies.

MAILING COOKIES

Packing cookies to mail is not too difficult if you remember two things: first, don't try to mail cookies that are very fragile unless you resign yourself to having them arrive in pieces; and second, remember to give any cookies plenty of cushioning for protection.

A tin box is ideal as it gives the greatest protection. Line it with wax paper, and provide plenty of crumpled or shredded wax paper to pack underneath, between, and on top of layers of cookies. I have been told that popcorn (popped, of course), sprinkled generously between layers, will bring cookies unbroken to a distant destination.

DROP COOKIES

CHOCOLATE ALMOND MACAROONS

Chewy tidbits you'll want to make often.

¾ cup sugar	5 ounces semisweet chocolate, grated or put through an electric blender
2 tablespoons water	
1 cup almonds, put through an electric blender	
	1 teaspoon vanilla extract
	3 egg whites

1. Butter a cooky sheet.

2. Mix sugar and water and stir over low heat to dissolve the sugar. Add the almonds and cool.

3. Mix in the grated chocolate, vanilla, and unbeaten egg whites.

4. Drop by spoonfuls onto the prepared cooky sheet.

Bake in a 350° F. oven for about 15 minutes. Cool on the cooky sheet before removing.

Makes about 2 dozen.

CHOCOLATE CHIP MERINGUES

2 egg whites	1 teaspoon vanilla extract
⅛ teaspoon cream of tartar	¾ cup semisweet chocolate
Pinch of salt	bits
¾ cup sugar	

1. Cover a cooky sheet with unglazed paper.

2. Beat egg whites until foamy throughout. Add cream of tartar and salt and beat until peaks are formed. Add sugar gradually, continuing to beat until very stiff. Fold in the vanilla and the chocolate bits. Drop by teaspoonfuls onto the prepared cooky sheet.

Bake in a 300° F. oven for 25 to 30 minutes.

Makes about 3 dozen.

CHOCOLATE CHIP ORANGE DROPS

¼ cup butter	½ teaspoon baking soda
¼ cup granulated sugar	2 tablespoons grated
¾ cup firmly packed brown	orange rind
sugar	½ cup ground almonds
1 egg	1 cup semisweet chocolate
1 teaspoon almond extract	bits
1 cup sifted flour	Orange Cheese Icing
¼ teaspoon salt	(pp. 119–120)

1. Butter cooky sheets lightly.

2. Cream butter and both sugars well and beat in the egg and almond extract.

3. Sift the flour, salt, and baking soda together. Add this, the grated rind, almonds, and chocolate bits. Mix. Drop by spoonfuls onto the cooky sheets, allowing room to spread.

Bake in a 375° F. oven for 10 to 12 minutes, or until the cookies begin to brown around the edges.

Remove to a cake rack to cool.

We like these brushed with Orange Cheese Icing.

Makes 3 dozen cookies.

CHOCOLATE COCONUT DAINTIES

They should be made small because of their extra richness.

⅓ cup sifted flour	2 ounces chocolate
⅔ cup sugar	(squares, melted and
½ teaspoon salt	cooled, or envelopes)
⅓ cup soft butter	1 tablespoon corn syrup
1 egg	1 tablespoon vanilla extract
	2½ cups grated coconut

1. Butter cooky sheets.

2. Sift flour, sugar, and salt into a mixing bowl. Add the butter, egg, chocolate, and corn syrup and blend on low speed. Stir in the vanilla and coconut.

3. Drop from a teaspoon onto the prepared cooky sheets.

Bake in a 350° F. oven for 8 to 10 minutes. Cool. Remove to cake rack.

Makes 3 to 4 dozen cookies.

CHOCOLATE FIG DROPS

This cooky keeps and freezes well.

½ cup butter
¾ cup firmly packed brown sugar
1 egg
1 teaspoon vanilla extract
½ cup chopped dried figs
½ cup semisweet chocolate bits

½ cup sifted flour
Pinch of salt
1 teaspoon ground cinnamon
½ teaspoon ground allspice
½ teaspoon ground cloves
1½ cups uncooked oatmeal

1. Butter cooky sheets.

2. Cream the butter and sugar until light and fluffy. Beat in the egg and the vanilla. Stir in the chopped figs and chocolate bits.

3. Sift the flour, salt, and spices. Beat this into the first mixture, and then add the oatmeal. Drop by teaspoons onto the cooky sheets.

Bake in a 325° F. oven for 15 minutes. Remove to racks and cool.

Makes 4 to 5 dozen.

CHOCOLATE FRUITCAKE NUGGETS

These are tasty little bits; the spicy cake blends with the chocolate topping for a delectable combination of flavors.

½ cup molasses
¼ cup water
1 box (15 ounces) seedless raisins
1 pound mixed candied fruits, chopped
½ cup butter
⅔ cup sugar
3 eggs
1 cup plus 2 tablespoons sifted flour
⅛ teaspoon baking soda
1 teaspoon ground cinnamon
1 teaspoon grated nutmeg
½ teaspoon ground allspice
¼ teaspoon ground cloves
4 tablespoons brandy
1½ cups broken pecan meats
Chocolate Glaze (p. 109)

1. Place paper baking cups into small muffin tins.

2. Put molasses, water, and raisins into a saucepan and bring to a boil. Simmer for 5 minutes. Add candied fruit. Cool.

3. Cream butter and sugar well. Add the eggs, one at a time, beating after each addition.

4. Sift flour, baking soda, and spices together and add alternately with the brandy. Add the molasses-raisin mixture and the pecans. Mix and spoon into baking cups.

Bake in a 325° F. oven for 25 minutes. Cool on cake racks.

Make Chocolate Glaze and drizzle on top of the nuggets.

Makes 40 to 50 cookies.

CHOCOLATE PECAN MERINGUES

Light as a cloud, a dark rich brown.

4 egg whites
⅛ teaspoon salt
¼ teaspoon cream of tartar
1 cup sugar
1 tablespoon vanilla extract

4 ounces chocolate (squares, melted and cooled, or envelopes)
1 cup pecan meats, finely ground or put through an electric blender

1. Butter cooky sheets.

2. Beat egg whites until foamy, add salt and cream of tartar, and add sugar gradually. Continue to beat until stiff peaks are formed. Fold in the vanilla, chocolate, and nut meats. Drop from a teaspoon onto the prepared cooky sheets.

Bake in a 350° F. oven for 15 to 18 minutes, or until cookies are no longer soft when touched lightly. Cool for a few minutes and then place on wire racks to cool.

To serve with ice cream topping, make large flat meringues. Pass your favorite Chocolate Sauce. (pp. 199–205).

Makes 3 to 4 dozen cookies.

CHOCOLATE RUM DROPS

30 small lumps of sugar
¼ cup dark rum
½ cup butter
1 cup firmly packed brown sugar
1 egg
1 teaspoon vanilla extract

2 ounces chocolate (squares, melted and cooled, or envelopes)
1¾ cups sifted flour
2 teaspoons baking powder
½ teaspoon salt
2 tablespoons milk

1. Butter cooky sheets.

2. Dip the sugar cubes quickly into the rum and set aside.

3. Cream the butter and sugar thoroughly. Beat in the egg, vanilla, and chocolate.

4. Sift the flour, baking powder, and salt. Add this alternately with the milk. Drop teaspoons onto the prepared sheets, allowing room to spread.

Bake in a 400° F. oven for 5 minutes.

5. Remove from the oven and put a sugar cube in the center of each cooky. Return to the oven for 3 or 4 minutes more. Cool on cake racks.

Makes 30 to 40 cookies.

FLORENTINES

There are several recipes for this elegant wafer, each differing slightly.

¼ cup butter
¼ cup brown sugar
1 tablespoon honey
½ cup sifted flour
½ cup candied fruits, cut up fine
½ cup candied lemon and orange peels, cut up fine

¼ cup chopped seedless raisins
½ cup almonds, ground or put through an electric blender
6 ounces semisweet chocolate, melted

1. Butter a cooky sheet.

2. Melt the butter and add the sugar and honey.

3. Sift the flour over the fruits and nuts, and add to the butter-sugar mixture. Mix well. Spoon small amounts onto the prepared cooky sheet and flatten each with a wet metal spatula.

Bake in a 350° F. oven for 8 to 10 minutes, or until the cookies are brown around the edges. Cool on a rack.

When cold, spread the bottoms with the melted chocolate.

Makes about 4 dozen cookies.

PORCUPINE COOKIES

4 egg whites
¼ teaspoon cream of tartar
⅛ teaspoon salt
1¼ cups sugar

¼ cup cocoa
1 teaspoon almond extract
1 cup slivered blanched almonds

1. Place unglazed brown paper on cooky sheets.

2. Whip egg whites until frothy and add the cream of tartar and salt. Beat until they stand in stiff peaks.

3. Mix sugar and cocoa and add gradually to the meringue. Add the almond extract. Drop from a teaspoon onto the paper-lined sheets. Stud the top of each cooky with 5 or 6 almond slivers.

Bake in a 300° F. oven for about 50 minutes, or until the almonds are toasted and the cookies dry. Cool on a wire cake rack.

Makes 3 to 4 dozen cookies.

SOUR-CREAM CHOCOLATE COOKIES

A rich, chocolatey nut cooky.

4 ounces chocolate
(squares, melted and cooled, or envelopes)
1 cup butter
2 cups firmly packed brown sugar
2 eggs
1 cup sour cream

1 teaspoon baking soda
3 cups sifted flour
½ teaspoon salt
1 teaspoon baking powder
1 tablespoon vanilla extract
1 cup broken walnut meats

1. Butter a cooky sheet.

2. Cream the butter and sugar. Add the eggs, one at a time, beating after each addition. Add the chocolate.

3. Mix the sour cream and baking soda.

4. Sift the flour, salt, and baking powder together, and beat in alternately with the sour cream. Add the vanilla and stir in the nut meats. Drop from a teaspoon onto the prepared cooky sheet, allowing room to spread.

Bake in a 375° F. oven for 8 to 10 minutes.

Makes 5 to 6 dozen cookies.

SOUR-MILK COCOA DROPS

½ cup butter	½ teaspoon baking soda
1 cup sugar	½ teaspoon salt
1 egg	½ cup sour milk
1 teaspoon vanilla extract	Vanilla Icing I (p. 124)
1¾ cups sifted flour	Pecan halves
⅔ cup cocoa	

1. Butter cooky sheets lightly.

2. Cream butter and sugar well. Beat in the egg and vanilla.

3. Sift the flour, cocoa, baking soda, and salt together. Add to the first mixture alternately with the sour milk. Drop by small spoonfuls onto the cooky sheets.

Bake in a 400° F. oven for 8 to 10 minutes. Cool on racks.

4. When cold, frost with Vanilla Icing, and press a pecan half on each. At Christmas time I use halves of glacéed cherries in place of the nuts.

Makes about 3 dozen.

SPICY CHOCOLATE OATMEAL DROPS

Another variation of that favorite, the chocolate chip cooky.

½ cup butter
1 cup sugar
2 eggs
2 teaspoons vanilla extract
½ cup plus 2 tablespoons sifted flour
¼ teaspoon salt

2 teaspoons ground cinnamon
½ teaspoon ground cloves
1½ cups uncooked oatmeal
1½ cups semisweet chocolate bits

1. Butter cooky sheets lightly and dust with flour.

2. Cream the butter and sugar together and beat in the eggs, one at a time, then the vanilla.

3. Sift the flour, salt, and spices together and add. Stir in the oatmeal. Mix well. Fold in the chocolate bits. Drop from a teaspoon onto the prepared cooky sheets.

Bake in a 375° F. oven for 15 to 20 minutes. Cool on cake racks.

Makes about 4 dozen cookies.

MOLDED COOKIES

ALMOND BALLS

¾ cup butter
¼ cup brown sugar
6 ounces semisweet chocolate, cut up, or 1 cup morsels
2 tablespoons heavy cream

1 teaspoon almond extract
2 cups sifted flour
Pinch of salt
½ teaspoon grated nutmeg
Almond halves, blanched
Rose Icing (p. 121)

1. Butter cooky sheets lightly.

2. Cream butter and sugar well.

3. Blend chocolate and cream over low heat until chocolate is melted. Add to the creamed mixture. Add the almond extract.

4. Sift flour, salt, and nutmeg together and add to the batter. Chill.

5. Shape into small balls and place on cooky sheets, flattening each one slightly.

Bake in a 350° F. oven for 12 to 15 minutes. Be careful not to overbake. Cool on racks.

6. When cold, ice with Rose Icing and press an almond half on top of each cooky.

Makes about 3 dozen cookies.

ALMOND WREATHS

These little cookies are unusual in that chopped almonds take the place of flour.

3 eggs	1 ounce chocolate, grated
1½ cups sugar	1 ounce semisweet choco-
Pinch of salt	late, grated
2 cups finely chopped blanched almonds	1 teaspoon almond extract

1. Butter a cooky sheet.

2. Beat the eggs until light and add the sugar gradually, beating as you add. Stir in the salt, nuts, both kinds of chocolate, and almond extract. Chill.

3. Shape the dough by hand into wreaths. Decorate with a bit of glacéed cherry if you like.

Bake in a 325° F. oven for about 15 minutes, or until very lightly browned. Remove to a rack to cool.

Makes about 2 dozen.

BRANDY BALLS

6 tablespoons cocoa
1 cup confectioners' sugar
2 cups chocolate-wafer crumbs (about 30 wafers)
1 cup finely chopped almonds
½ teaspoon ground cloves
2 tablespoons light corn syrup
⅓ cup brandy

1. Mix 4 tablespoons of the cocoa and the sugar. Add the chocolate-wafer crumbs, almonds, and cloves. Stir to mix well.

2. Blend the corn syrup and brandy and stir into the first mixture, mixing thoroughly. Shape into balls, roll in the remaining cocoa, and store in an airtight box between layers of wax paper. Allow to ripen for a few days before using.

Makes about 4 dozen.

CHOCOLATE ALMOND BUTTER BALLS

These creamy confections are the best ever. Serve with sherry or mulled wine at Christmas time.

¼ pound (½ cup) butter
3 tablespoons confectioners' sugar
⅔ cup sifted flour
¼ cup cocoa
1 cup toasted blanched almonds, ground fine or put through an electric blender
Confectioners' sugar, sifted

1. Cream the butter well. Add the 3 tablespoons sugar and cream again.

2. Mix the flour and cocoa and beat into the creamed mixture. Add the almonds and mix well. Chill.

3. Roll into small balls and place 2 inches apart on an ungreased cooky sheet.

Bake in a 325° F. oven for about 20 minutes.

4. Remove from the baking sheet and roll in confectioners' sugar. Cool on cake racks.

Makes 3 to 4 dozen cookies, depending on the size.

CHOCOLATE CHERRIES

An attractive addition to the tea tray.

1 cup butter	2½ cups sifted flour
¾ cup sugar	1 teaspoon ground cinnamon
2 eggs, separated	mon
2 ounces chocolate (squares, melted and cooled, or envelopes)	½ teaspoon salt
	1½ cups blanched almonds, finely ground or grated in an electric blender
1 tablespoon vanilla extract	
	Glacéed cherry halves

1. Cream butter and sugar well. Beat in the egg yolks, then the chocolate and vanilla.

2. Sift flour, cinnamon, and salt together and add to the batter. Chill.

3. Shape into small balls. Roll each one in the slightly beaten egg white and then in the ground almonds. Press a cherry half on each one.

Bake in a 450° F. oven for 12 to 15 minutes, or until lightly browned. Cool on rack.

Makes 4 to 5 dozen cookies.

CHOCOLATE ROSES

This delicately flavored cooky is beautiful as well as delicious.

1 cup butter
⅔ cup sugar
3 egg yolks
½ teaspoon rose flavoring

A drop or two of red food coloring
2 cups sifted flour
2 ounces (squares) semi-sweet chocolate, melted

1. Cream the butter and sugar until light. Add the egg yolks and beat until creamy. Add the rose flavoring and enough coloring to make the dough a delicate pink. Beat in the flour a little at a time.

2. Press onto an unbuttered cooky sheet, using any tip for your cooky press that will make a cooky resembling a flower.

Bake at 375° F. for 8 to 10 minutes. Remove to cake racks to cool.

3. When cold, brush petals lightly around the edges with the melted chocolate.

Makes 50 to 60 cookies.

CHOCOLATE SPRITZ COOKIES

A Spritz cooky, rich in butter and eggs, is a must at Christmas time. This chocolate version is a welcome treat at any season. You need a cooky press or a pastry bag with a tip that forms stars.

1 cup butter
⅔ cup sugar
3 egg yolks
2 ounces chocolate
   (squares, melted and
   cooled, or envelopes)

½ teaspoon vanilla extract
2½ cups sifted flour
   (about)

1. Butter a baking sheet very lightly.

2. Cream the butter and sugar together; add the egg yolks, one at a time, beating after each addition. Add the chocolate. Stir in the vanilla. Beat in enough flour to make a soft dough which can be pressed through a pastry tube into wreaths or "S"s.

Bake in a 400° F. oven for about 8 minutes. Allow to cool slightly before removing to a cake rack. These must be handled carefully, as they are very delicate.

Makes 60 to 70 cookies.

Variation: CHOCOLATE-TOPPED SPRITZ COOKIES

Omit the chocolate from the above recipe.

Melt semisweet chocolate and drizzle back and forth over the tops of the baked and cooled cookies.

CHOCOLATE WALNUT DELIGHTS

¾ cup butter	1¾ cups sifted flour
1 cup firmly packed brown sugar	2 teaspoons baking soda
1 egg	¼ teaspoon salt
¼ cup corn syrup	½ teaspoon ground cinnamon
3 ounces chocolate (squares, melted and cooled, or envelopes)	½ teaspoon ground allspice
	¼ teaspoon grated nutmeg
	Walnut halves

1. Cream the butter and sugar together until creamy. Add the egg and beat well. Add the corn syrup and the cooled chocolate.

2. Sift the flour, baking soda, salt, and spices together, and beat into the first mixture. Chill.

3. Roll into small balls, place on unbuttered cooky sheets, and press a walnut half on each cooky. Allow room between the cookies as they will spread as they bake.

Bake in a 350° F. oven for about 15 minutes. Allow to cool slightly before removing to cake racks.

Makes 30 to 36 cookies.

CHRISTMAS WREATHS

Decorate these with bits of glacéed cherries or angelica to add the Christmas colors.

1 cup butter
¾ cup plus 2 tablespoons confectioners' sugar
1 egg, separated
1 extra egg yolk
1 tablespoon brandy
1 teaspoon almond extract

2 cups sifted flour
Pinch of salt
1 tablespoon cocoa
4 tablespoons blanched almonds, put through an electric blender

1. Cream the butter and ¾ cup sugar well. Add the egg yolks and beat again. Add the brandy and almond extract.

2. Sift the flour with the salt, and mix in. This dough will be quite stiff and you may have to knead it in at the end. Press onto an unbuttered cooky sheet, using a cooky press or a pastry bag, making wreaths or rings.

3. Beat the egg white a little, and brush the wreaths lightly with this. Mix the remaining sugar, the cocoa, and almonds and dust the tops with this mixture.

Bake for 10 minutes in a 350° F. oven. Be careful not to overbake, as the flavor is better if they do not brown.

Makes 50 to 60 cookies.

CINNAMON CHOCOLATE DIPS

A delicate cooky, irresistible in flavor.

1 cup butter
¾ cup sugar
1 egg
1 teaspoon vanilla extract
2½ cups sifted flour

2 teaspoons ground cinnamon
½ teaspoon salt
Melted semisweet chocolate
Finely ground walnuts

1. Cream the butter and sugar together. Add the egg and beat well. Stir in the vanilla.

2. Sift the flour, cinnamon, and salt together. Gradually beat into the batter. Fill a cooky press, using a tip that will form rectangular cookies, about 1 inch by 2 inches. Press onto an ungreased cooky sheet.

Bake in a 375° F. oven for 12 to 15 minutes. Remove to a cake rack to cool. When cold, dip about an inch of the end of each cooky into the melted chocolate and then into the chopped nuts.

Makes about 4 dozen cookies.

CINNAMON CRESCENTS

A delicious addition to your assortment of Christmas cookies.

½ pound almond paste	1 cup blanched almonds,
½ cup confectioners' sugar	finely ground or put
½ teaspoon ground cinnamon	through an electric
mon	blender
1 egg white	Bittersweet Chocolate
	Frosting (p. 104)
	Cinnamon candies

1. Butter cooky sheet.

2. Mix all the ingredients except almonds thoroughly. Roll in a long roll. Cut off pieces about 1 inch long. Shape each one into a crescent and roll it in the ground nuts. Place on the prepared sheet.

Bake in a 300° F. oven for 20 minutes. Cool.

Frost with Bittersweet Chocolate Frosting and top each cooky with a cinnamon candy.

Makes 1½ to 2 dozen.

SURPRISE NUGGETS

Use your ingenuity to vary the filling of these dainty morsels.

½ cup butter
¾ cup confectioners' sugar
1 tablespoon rum
1½ cups sifted flour

Pinch of salt
Glossy Chocolate Frosting
  (p. 118)
Glacéed cherries

1. Cream butter and sugar well. Add rum, then the flour and salt. The dough will be very stiff and you may have to knead in the last bit of flour.

2. Wrap a cherry in enough dough to cover it completely. Place the nuggets on an unbuttered cooky sheet.

Bake in a 350° F. oven for 10 to 12 minutes.

Frost with Glossy Chocolate Frosting or any chocolate frosting and decorate the tops with bits of cherry.

Makes 2 to 3 dozen.

ROLLED COOKIES

CHOCOLATE SANDWICH COOKIES

½ pound (1 cup) butter
1 cup sugar
1 whole egg
2 extra egg yolks
1 teaspoon almond extract
1 tablespoon brandy

2 teaspoons grated lemon
  rind
1½ cups cornstarch
½ cup sifted flour
1 teaspoon baking powder
Coffee Rum and Butter
  Frosting (p. 114)

1. Cream butter and sugar well. Add the egg and the egg yolks, one at a time, beating after each addition. Stir in the flavorings and the lemon rind.

2. Sift the dry ingredients. Add to the rest, mixing well. You will find this very stiff. Turn out on a board and knead until smooth. Chill.

3. Roll out the dough to about ½-inch thickness. Cut into any shapes you desire.

Bake in a 350° F. oven for 10 to 12 minutes, or until the cookies are light brown and spring back when touched lightly.

4. Make Coffee Rum and Butter Frosting and put the cookies together in pairs.

Makes about 2 dozen double cookies.

CHOCOLATE WAFERS

These are thin and crisp and melt in the mouth.

1½ tablespoons butter	¼ cup cocoa
½ cup sugar	⅛ teaspoon salt
1 egg	1 teaspoon baking powder
1 teaspoon vanilla extract	3 tablespoons milk
½ cup sifted flour	

1. Butter cooky sheets and dust them with cocoa.

2. Cream the butter and sugar well. Beat in the egg and the vanilla.

3. Sift the flour, cocoa, salt, and baking powder together and add this alternately with the milk. Drop by teaspoonfuls on the prepared cooky sheets, allowing room for spreading.

Bake in a 350° F. oven for about 7 minutes.

Makes 2 to 3 dozen cookies.

CHOCOLATE WAFER CREAMS

3 ounces chocolate (squares, melted, or envelopes)
½ cup butter
1¼ cups sugar
2 eggs
1 tablespoon vanilla extract
2 cups sifted flour

1½ teaspoons baking powder
½ teaspoon baking soda
¼ teaspoon salt
Chocolate Butter Icing (pp. 106–107) or Black and White Peppermint Frosting (p. 104)

1. Cream the butter and sugar until light and fluffy. Add the eggs and beat, then add the chocolate and the vanilla.

2. Sift the flour, baking powder, baking soda, and salt together. Beat into the first mixture gradually. Chill.

3. Roll out the dough very thin on a lightly floured board, and cut with a scalloped or other cooky cutter. Put the cookies on an unbuttered cooky sheet, allowing room for them to spread.

Bake at 350° F. for 8 to 10 minutes. Allow to cool slightly before removing to cake racks. When cold, put the cookies together with Chocolate Butter Icing or Black and White Peppermint Frosting.

Makes 30 to 36 sandwich cookies.

CHRISTMAS HEARTS

Use your creative imagination in frosting and decorating these festive little hearts.

½ cup butter
½ cup molasses
½ cup honey
½ cup sour milk

4 cups sifted flour (about)
¼ cup cocoa
½ teaspoon baking soda
¼ teaspoon salt

1. Butter cooky sheets and dust them with cocoa.

2. Cream the butter and slowly add the molasses and honey, beating as you pour. Then beat in the sour milk.

3. Sift 3 cups of the flour with the cocoa, baking soda, and salt. Beat well into the first mixture. Add enough of the remaining cup of flour to make a dough stiff enough to roll out. Chill.

4. Roll out ⅓-inch thick on a lightly floured board. Cut with a heart-shaped cutter. Place on the prepared cooky sheets.

Bake in a 350° F. oven for about 15 minutes.

Ice, then decorate with glacéed fruits and nuts or colored icing put through a pastry tube.

Makes 3 to 4 dozen hearts.

COCOA STARS

This is a variation of Cinnamon Stars, traditionally made at Christmas time.

7 egg whites
1 pound (3½ cups) confectioners' sugar
1 teaspoon ground cinnamon

2 tablespoons cocoa
1 pound blanched almonds, put through an electric blender
Cinnamon drops (optional)

1. Butter cooky sheets lightly.

2. Beat the egg whites until stiff and add the sugar gradually, beating as you add. (The old recipes assure you that 30 minutes is not too long, but I have never done this. Just beat until very stiff.) Beat in the cinnamon and take out about ½ cup of this meringue mixture, reserving it to ice the stars.

3. Beat in the cocoa and then fold in the almonds. Dust the pastry board with sifted confectioners' sugar or sugar and cocoa mixed. Roll out the dough about ⅓-inch thick, cut into stars, and place the stars on prepared cooky sheets. Allow to stand overnight to form a crust.

4. Spread a little of the reserved meringue on each star. You may add a cinnamon drop (redhot) if you wish.

Bake in a 325° F. oven for 15 minutes. Cool on wire racks.

Makes about 4 dozen cookies.

REFRIGERATOR COOKIES

BLACK WALNUT CRISPS

A thin but rich cooky—the chocolate topping enhances the special flavor of the black walnuts.

1 cup butter	1 teaspoon baking powder
2 cups firmly packed brown sugar	1 cup black walnut meats, chopped
2 eggs	2 cups semisweet chocolate bits, melted
4 cups sifted flour	
Pinch of salt	

1. Cream butter and sugar together. Add the eggs, one at a time, beating after each addition.

2. Sift the flour, salt, and baking powder together and beat into the first mixture. This will become very stiff. Work the nut meats in and shape the dough into a roll about 1½ inches in diameter. Wrap in wax paper and chill in refrigerator overnight.

3. Cut the roll into slices ⅛-inch thick and place them on an unbuttered cooky sheet.

Bake in a 375° F. oven for 8 to 10 minutes, or until lightly browned. Cool on racks.

5. When cold, brush tops with the melted chocolate. Allow the chocolate to harden before storing.

Makes about 5 dozen cookies.

CHOCOLATE-ALMOND REFRIGERATOR COOKIES

½ cup butter
1 cup sugar
1 egg
1 teaspoon almond extract
2 ounces chocolate (squares, melted and cooled, or envelopes)

2 cups sifted flour
2 teaspoons baking powder
½ teaspoon salt
1 cup chopped toasted almonds

1. Cream the butter and sugar. Beat in the egg, almond extract, and chocolate.

2. Sift the flour, baking powder, and salt. Add to the first mixture, beating well. Stir in the nuts.

3. Shape into a roll about 1½ inches in diameter. Wrap in wax paper and refrigerate overnight.

4. Slice thinly and place on ungreased cooky sheets.

Bake in a 350° F. oven for 10 to 12 minutes. Cool on racks.

Makes about 4 dozen cookies.

CHOCOLATE CHERRY SLICES

½ cup butter
¾ cup confectioners' sugar
Pinch of salt
1 teaspoon almond extract
1 teaspoon vanilla extract

1½ cups sifted flour
1 cup glacéed cherries
1 cup semisweet chocolate bits, melted

1. Cream butter and sugar well. Add the salt and almond and vanilla extracts.

2. Beat in the flour and then add the cherries. The batter will be very stiff. Form into a roll, wrap in foil, and chill in the refrigerator overnight.

3. Slice thinly and place on ungreased cooky sheets.

Bake in a 400° F. oven for 8 to 10 minutes. Cool and remove to wire racks. Brush with the melted chocolate.

Makes about 3 dozen cookies.

CHOCOLATE PEANUT REFRIGERATOR CRISPS

1 cup semisweet chocolate bits, melted and cooled
½ cup peanut butter
1½ cups confectioners' sugar
1 tablespoon butter
2 teaspoons instant coffee powder
½ cup boiling water
1 egg
1 tablespoon vanilla extract
½ cup chocolate-wafer crumbs

1. Butter cooky sheets.

2. Mix the chocolate, peanut butter, sugar, butter, coffee powder, and boiling water. Blend and cool.

3. Beat the egg well, add the vanilla, chocolate crumbs, and cooled chocolate mixture. Mix thoroughly. Roll, wrap in foil, and refrigerate.

4. Cut into ¼-inch slices and place on the prepared cooky sheets. Bake at 350° F. for 10 to 15 minutes.

Makes 2 to 3 dozen cookies.

ALMOND BROT

A delicious little cake with a foreign air.

2 eggs
1 cup firmly packed brown sugar
1 ounce (1 square) chocolate, grated
1 cup unblanched almonds, coarsely chopped

1 teaspoon baking powder
½ teaspoon ground cinnamon
2 cups sifted flour
1 teaspoon vanilla extract

1. Butter a 9-inch-square baking pan.

2. Beat the eggs until light and then add the sugar gradually, beating well. Stir in the chocolate and almonds, then the dry ingredients, sifted together, and the vanilla. Mix well and press into the prepared pan.

Bake in a 350° F. oven for 25 minutes. Cool slightly and cut into strips.

Makes about 2 dozen.

BUTTERSCOTCH BARS WITH CHOCOLATE NUT TOPPING

½ cup butter
½ cup firmly packed brown sugar
1 teaspoon vanilla extract
1 egg
½ cup sifted flour

¼ teaspoon salt
½ cup uncooked oatmeal
1½ cups semisweet chocolate bits, melted
¾ cup broken pecan meats

1. Butter a 9-inch-square baking pan.

2. Cream butter and sugar well, add the vanilla, and beat in the egg. Beat in the flour and salt. Then stir in the oatmeal. Spread the batter in the prepared pan.

Bake at 350° F. for 20 to 25 minutes. Cool slightly.

3. Spread the melted chocolate on top, and sprinkle with the nuts. When set, cut into bars.

Makes 2 dozen bars.

CHEWY NUT STICKS

A delectably rich cooky, easy to make.

¼ pound (½ cup) butter
1 cup vanilla-wafer crumbs
1 cup dried currants
1 cup semisweet chocolate bits

1 cup chopped walnuts
1 can (15 ounces) condensed (sweet) milk

1. Melt the butter in a 9-inch-square baking pan.

2. Spread vanilla wafer crumbs on top. Sprinkle with the currants, then the chocolate bits, and finally the nuts. Pour the condensed milk evenly over the top.

Bake in a 350° F. oven for 30 minutes. Cool in the pan and cut into bars. This will make 30 to 36 bars, depending on the size. I like to make them rather small, as they are so rich.

CHOCOLATE FILBERT SQUARES

½ cup butter
3 ounces chocolate (squares, melted, or envelopes)
1 cup firmly packed brown sugar

2 eggs
½ cup sifted flour
Pinch of salt
1 tablespoon vanilla extract
36 filbert (or hazelnut) halves

1. Butter a 9-inch-square baking pan.

2. Blend the butter and chocolate over hot water. Stir in the sugar, and beat in the eggs, one at a time. Add the flour, salt, and vanilla. Pour into the prepared pan, spreading evenly. Place the nuts so that when the bars are cut into squares, each square will have a nut in the center.

Bake in a 400° F. oven for 10 to 12 minutes. Cool slightly. Cut into squares.

Makes 64 cookies.

CHOCOLATE FRUIT SQUARES

These delectable little tidbits will keep well, and they are good to have in the freezer, too.

Crust

1 cup sifted flour	¼ cup sugar
Few grains of salt	½ cup butter

Sift the flour, salt, and sugar together, and cut in the butter with a pastry blender. Pat firmly into an 8-inch-square baking pan.

Bake in a 350° F. oven for 15 minutes.

Make the filling.

Filling

3 eggs	1 cup fruit, cut up
1 cup firmly packed brown sugar	(cooked prunes or canned figs)
1 teaspoon vanilla extract	½ cup semisweet chocolate bits
⅓ cup flour	
½ teaspoon baking powder	Confectioners' sugar, sifted
Pinch of salt	

1. Beat the eggs well. Beat in the sugar and vanilla.

2. Sift the flour, baking powder, and salt together. Stir gradually into the egg-sugar mixture, blending thoroughly. Fold in the fruit, then the chocolate bits. Pour this over the warm pastry, spreading evenly. Dust with confectioners' sugar.

Bake in a 350° F. oven for 30 minutes.

Cool and cut into small squares. To serve as a dessert, cut into larger squares, and top with whipped cream.

Makes 16 to 36 squares, according to size.

CHOCOLATE HONEY SQUARES

¼ cup butter
¾ cup sugar
¼ cup honey
2 eggs
3 ounces chocolate
(squares, melted and cooled, or envelopes)

½ cup sifted flour
½ teaspoon salt
1 teaspoon vanilla extract
1 cup chopped walnuts
Broiled Almond Frosting (p. 105), made with walnuts

1. Butter a 9-inch-square baking pan.

2. Cream butter and sugar well. Add the honey. Beat in the eggs, one at a time, and then the chocolate. Add the flour, salt, and vanilla. Mix well and stir in the nuts. Spread into the prepared pan.

Bake in a 350° F. oven for 25 to 30 minutes. Make Broiled Almond Frosting, using walnuts instead of almonds. Spread it over the baked dough and brown briefly under the broiler. Cool and cut into squares.

Makes 36 squares.

CHOCOLATE MERINGUE SQUARES

1½ cups chocolate-wafer crumbs (about 30 wafers)
½ cup plus 2 tablespoons sugar

4 tablespoons butter
Seedless raspberry jam
4 egg whites
½ teaspoon almond extract

1. Mix the crumbs and 2 tablespoons of the sugar. Cut the butter into the mixture with a pastry blender. Press all firmly into the bottom of the 8 x 8 x 2-inch-square baking pan. Spread a layer of jam on top.

2. Whip the egg whites until foamy throughout. Add the ½ cup of sugar, a teaspoon at a time, beating as you add. Add the almond extract. Beat until very stiff. Spread the meringue over the jam.

Bake in a 325° F. oven for 12 to 15 minutes, or until slightly brown.

Makes 16 two-inch squares.

CHOCOLATE NUT FINGERS

An exceptionally delicious dark, chewy bar which has that richly satisfying chocolate flavor.

3 egg whites
1½ cups confectioners' sugar
3 ounces chocolate (squares, melted and cooled, or envelopes)

1 cup blanched almonds, finely ground or put through an electric blender
1 tablespoon vanilla extract

1. Butter a 9-inch-square cake pan and dust it with cocoa.

2. Beat the egg whites until stiff, and beat in the sugar gradually. Fold in the cooled chocolate, half of the almonds, and the vanilla.

3. Spread in the prepared pan, and sprinkle the rest of the nuts on top.

Bake in a 300° F. oven for 20 to 25 minutes. Cool, and cut into bars.

Makes about 27 bars.

CHOCOLATE CHEESE LAYERS

A delectable layered bar, with cream cheese one of its ingredients

8 ounces cream cheese
1½ cups firmly packed brown sugar
½ cup butter
3 eggs
4 ounces unsweetened chocolate (squares, melted and cooled, or envelopes)
1½ cups sifted flour
⅛ teaspoon salt
1 teaspoon baking powder
1 tablespoon vanilla extract
1 cup broken pecan meats

1. Butter a 9-inch-square cake pan. Dust it with cocoa.

2. Beat half of the cream cheese (4 ounces) with ½ cup of the brown sugar. Set aside.

3. Cream the rest of the sugar (1 cup) with the butter. Add the remaining cream cheese (4 ounces). Beat in the eggs, one at a time. Add the cooled chocolate.

4. Sift the flour, salt, and baking powder together. Add this and the vanilla to the egg-chocolate mixture. Fold in half (½ cup) of the pecan meats. Spread half of the batter in the prepared pan. Cover this with the cream-cheese and brown-sugar mixture. Then spread the rest of the batter on top. Sprinkle the remaining pecans on top.

Bake in a 350° F. oven for 25 minutes. Allow to cool before cutting into squares or bars.

Makes about 2 dozen cookies.

CHRISTMAS SPICE SQUARES

A delectable combination of chocolate and molasses, set off by a tart glaze. These keep very well.

¼ cup butter
½ cup sugar
3 eggs
2 tablespoons brandy
⅓ cup molasses
1 cup sifted flour
1 teaspoon baking powder
1 teaspoon ground cinnamon

¼ teaspoon ground allspice
¼ teaspoon ground cloves
1 ounce (square) unsweetened chocolate, grated
⅓ cup chopped citron
⅔ cup broken pecan meats
Lemon Glaze (p. 119)

1. Butter a 9-inch-square baking pan and line it with wax paper.

2. Cream the butter and sugar well. Add the eggs, one at a time, beating after each addition. Then beat in the brandy and molasses.

3. Sift the flour, baking powder, and spices together, and add. Then fold in the grated chocolate, the citron and nuts. Spread evenly in the prepared pan.

Bake in a 350° F. oven until the cake shrinks slightly from the sides of the pan. Do not allow it to bake so long that it becomes dry. Turn out on a cake rack.

When cool, cut into squares and ice with Lemon Glaze. Let this harden before packing in an airtight box.

Makes 36 squares.

DANISH CHOCOLATE BARS

The most delicious dark chocolate cookies you ever ate.

4 ounces chocolate (squares, melted and cooled, or envelopes)
6 tablespoons butter
2 tablespoons sugar
3 eggs, separated
1 teaspoon vanilla extract
¾ cup sifted flour
1 teaspoon baking powder
Pinch of salt
¼ cup milk
½ cup chopped, toasted almonds
2 ounces unsweetened chocolate, (squares, melted)
Vanilla Icing II (p. 124)

1. Butter an 8-inch-square pan and dust it with cocoa.

2. Cream the butter, add the sugar, and beat. Add the egg yolks, one at a time, beating after each addition. Add the melted chocolate and the vanilla.

3. Sift the dry ingredients together, and add alternately with the milk.

4. Beat the egg whites until stiff but not dry. Fold gently into the batter. Fold in the nuts. Spread the batter into the prepared pan.

Bake in a 350° F. oven for 30 minutes, or until the cake shrinks from the sides of the pan. Cool in the pan for 15 minutes.

Turn out on cake rack to cool completely. When cold, ice with Vanilla Icing. Melt the remaining 2 squares of chocolate and spread quickly over the icing when it has set sufficiently. Cut into bars.

Makes 32 bars.

DIXIE BROWNIES

If you enjoy a really spicy brownie, this is it.

2 ounces chocolate (squares, melted, or envelopes)
¼ cup melted butter
⅓ cup molasses
½ cup sugar
3 tablespoons grated orange rind
1 egg

1 cup flour
1 teaspoon baking powder
¼ teaspoon ground allspice
½ teaspoon ground cinnamon
¼ teaspoon ground cloves
¼ teaspoon salt
1 cup chopped pecans
Caramel Glaze (p. 106)

1. Butter a 9-inch-square baking pan and dust it with cocoa.

2. Blend the chocolate, butter, molasses, and sugar. Add the orange rind and egg.

3. Sift the flour, baking powder, spices, and salt together. Beat into the batter a little at a time. Stir in the nuts. Spread the batter in the prepared pan.

Bake in a 325° F. oven for 15 to 20 minutes. Turn out on a cake rack to cool. Cut into squares. Caramel Glaze is good on these.

Makes 36 brownies.

BROWNIES, WHOLE-WHEAT

Made with stone-ground whole-wheat flour, these brownies have a hearty richness. If stone-ground is not available, use any good whole-wheat flour.

½ cup butter
1 cup sugar
2 eggs
1 teaspoon vanilla extract
¾ cup stone-ground whole-wheat flour
½ teaspoon baking powder

Pinch of salt
3 ounces unsweetened chocolate (squares, melted and cooled, or envelopes)
1 cup coarsely chopped walnuts

1. Butter an 8-inch-square baking pan.

2. Cream butter and sugar till light and fluffy. Beat in the eggs, one at a time, and then the vanilla.

3. Mix the whole-wheat flour, baking powder, and salt. Beat into the first mixture. Stir in the chocolate. Fold in the nuts. Spread in the prepared pan.

Bake in a 350° F. oven for 20 minutes. Cool. Cut into squares.

Makes 16 to 36 squares, according to size.

FROSTED SHORTBREAD SQUARES

Shortbread is one of the most delectable creations in the cooky family. The flavor of orange makes this special.

2 cups butter	4 cups flour
1 cup firmly packed brown sugar	1½ cups semisweet chocolate bits
1 egg yolk	1 tablespoon butter
Few grains of salt	Candied orange peel, chopped fine
1 tablespoon grated orange rind	

1. Butter two 9-inch-square baking pans.

2. Cream the butter and sugar well. Beat in the egg yolk, salt, orange rind, and flour. This will make a very stiff dough that you may have to knead in order to incorporate all the flour. Press into the prepared pans. Prick all over with a fork.

Bake in a 325° F. oven for 25 to 30 minutes.

3. Melt the chocolate and blend it with the butter. Brush the mixture over the hot dough. Sprinkle the finely chopped orange rind on top, gently pressing it into the chocolate. Cut into squares before the chocolate sets.

Makes about 6 dozen squares.

CHOCOLATE SHORTBREAD

1 cup soft butter	1½ cups sifted flour
1 cup sugar	½ cup cocoa

1. Cream the butter and add the sugar.

2. Sift the flour and cocoa together and add to the above creamed mixture.

3. Roll or pat out on a lightly floured board to about ½-inch thick. Cut with a small cooky cutter and place on an unbuttered cooky sheet. Prick the tops of the cookies with the tines of a fork.

Bake in a 350° F. oven for 20 to 25 minutes. Cool on cake racks.

Makes about 24 cookies.

HEAVENLY ALMOND BARS

A delicious blend of nuts and chocolate make this rich filled bar.

Cooky Dough

½ cup butter	½ cup almonds, put through
¼ cup sugar	an electric blender or
1 egg	finely chopped
1½ cups sifted flour	1 teaspoon almond extract
2 ounces chocolate (squares, melted and cooled, or envelopes)	

1. Butter a 9-inch-square pan.

2. Cream the butter and sugar well, and beat in the egg. Then add the flour, the cooled chocolate, the almonds and almond extract.

3. Pat or press half of this into the bottom of the prepared pan. Chill the rest while you make the filling.

⅓ cup sugar
¾ cup almonds finely ground or put through an electric blender

1 tablespoon dark rum
1 egg white

1. Mix the sugar and almonds, then add the rum and the unbeaten egg white. Mix thoroughly. Spread this on the dough in the pan.

2. Roll out the chilled dough to fit the pan, and place this on top of the filling.

Bake in a 350° F. oven for about 40 minutes. Cut into bars while hot.

Makes 27 bars.

LEBKUCHEN

Traditional Christmas cakes are of many sizes and differ in ingredients; ours are enhanced by a chocolate icing.

2¾ cups sifted flour
½ teaspoon baking soda
½ teaspoon salt
1 teaspoon grated nutmeg
1 teaspoon ground cloves
1 teaspoon ground allspice

1 cup honey
¾ cup sugar
1 egg
1 cup chopped candied fruit
Chocolate Glaze (p. 108)

1. Butter an 8-inch-square baking pan.

2. Sift flour, baking soda, salt, and spices together.

3. Mix honey and sugar. Bring to a boil, remove from the heat, and cool.

4. Beat the eggs into the cooled molasses, then add the dry ingredients and the fruit. Press in to the bottom of the prepared pan.

Bake in a 400° F. oven for 12 to 15 minutes. Make Chocolate Glaze and spread or brush it over the warm cake. Cool. Cut into bars 2 inches by 1 inch.

Makes 32 cookies.

ORANGE BROWNIES

Here we use candied orange peel for a pleasantly different chocolate brownie.

½ cup butter
1 cup firmly packed brown sugar
3 ounces chocolate (squares, melted and cooled, or envelopes)
2 eggs
1 tablespoon vanilla extract

1 cup sifted flour
¼ teaspoon baking powder
¼ teaspoon salt
½ cup chopped candied orange peel
1 cup chopped almonds
Almond halves

1. Butter a 9-inch-square cake pan.

2. Cream butter and sugar well. Stir in the cooled chocolate. Beat in the eggs, one at a time, and the vanilla.

3. Sift the flour, baking powder, and salt together. Add to the batter, beating well. Stir in the orange peel and chopped almonds.

Spread the batter evenly in the prepared pan, pressing in an almond half at intervals so that one will center each square when the brownies are cut.

Bake at 350° F. for 50 minutes. Cool in the pan. Cut into squares.

Makes 36 brownies.

RICH CHOCOLATE COCONUT SQUARES

4 ounces chocolate (squares, melted, or envelopes)
1 cup sugar
2 egg whites
1 cup grated coconut
¼ cup sifted flour
½ teaspoon baking powder
¼ teaspoon salt
1 tablespoon vanilla extract
½ cup broken walnut meats

1. Butter a 9-inch-square pan.

2. Combine the chocolate, sugar, and unbeaten egg whites. Add the coconut. Cook over low heat, stirring, until the mixture is heated through.

3. Sift the flour, baking powder, and salt together and add. Stir in the vanilla and the nuts. Spread in the prepared pan.

Bake at 350° F. for 20 minutes. Cool and cut into squares

Makes about 3 dozen squares. They are rich, so you may want to cut them smaller.

PIES AND PIECRUSTS

*T*HERE ARE so many different kinds of piecrusts to choose from, that it makes a decision difficult.

The standard pastry crust is always delicious. Flaky and tender, it blends with the filling, chocolate or any other, you may put in it. If you are a real chocolate fan, you will prefer the chocolate-wafer crust, or perhaps the semisweet chocolate shell. The addition of nuts to a pastry adds a richness and a delectable flavor to any pie. Use almond flavoring, vanilla, cinnamon, or nutmeg; experiment and see how each addition changes the flavor with delightful results.

PIECRUSTS

PASTRY FOR A TWO-CRUST PIE

You will not find these proportions of ingredients in most cookbooks, but I find them the best ever—tender and foolproof. At times you may find the pastry a little hard to handle without breaking, but this is easily overlooked because of its other virtues. A French rolling pin makes rolling a piecrust a breeze. Try it.

2 cups all-purpose flour	1 cup shortening
1 teaspoon salt	Cold water

1. Mix flour, salt, and shortening with a pastry blender. Add enough cold water to just hold it all together. Too much water makes a tough crust, so add it carefully.

2. Roll out on a slightly floured board.

For a baked pie shell, use half the amount above. Prick all over with a fork and bake in a 475° F. oven for 8 to 10 minutes, or until the crust is a delicate brown. Watch it carefully, as it can become too brown very quickly. Cool before filling.

Variation: PECAN PASTRY

Substitute pecan meats, put through an electric blender or finely ground, for half of the shortening in your favorite pastry recipe.

Variation: SESAME-SEED PASTRY

Mix 2 or 3 tablespoons toasted sesame seeds with the flour when you make a pastry shell. It adds an interesting nutty flavor.

PASTRY MADE IN A MIXER

(for a 2-crust pie)

2 cups flour (all-purpose   1 cup shortening
  or instant)   ¼ cup cold water
1 teaspoon salt

Sift flour and salt into a mixing bowl. Add the shortening and blend at low speed. Add the cold water and mix for 15 seconds, or until the pastry forms a ball. Roll out, fit into the pan, and bake, following the directions for pastry (p. 249).

PASTRY MADE WITH OIL

(for a 2-crust pie)

2 cups flour   3 tablespoons cold water
1 teaspoon salt
½ cup salad oil

1. Put flour and salt in a bowl. Add the oil and mix with a fork. Add the water and mix that in. If the pastry seems too dry, a little more oil may be added. Roll out half of the pastry between 2 pieces of wax paper. Place in an 8- or 9-inch pie pan.

2. Put the filling in the pie. Dampen the edge of the pastry slightly.

3. Roll out the rest of the pastry as above, cut slits for the escape of steam, and fit this crust on top of the filling. Crimp around the edge of the pie.

Bake according to directions given with the pie recipe.

PEANUT PASTRY

Wonderful for chocolate cream pie.

(for a 1-crust pie)

1 cup flour
½ teaspoon baking powder
Pinch of salt
⅓ cup shortening

4 tablespoons smooth peanut butter
Cold water (a few tablespoons)

Sift the flour, baking powder, and salt together. Cut in the shortening and the peanut butter with a pastry blender. Add just enough water to make it stick together. Chill. Roll out the pastry, fit it into the pan, and bake following the directions for a pie shell (p. 249).

PASTRY SHELLS

ALMOND PASTRY SHELL

Make half of the recipe for Pastry (p. 249), adding 1 teaspoon almond extract to the dry ingredients. Sprinkle chopped or slivered toasted almonds on the pastry before baking. Bake, following the directions for the baked pie shell (p. 249), and cool. Fill with any chocolate filling.

CHOCOLATE PASTRY SHELL

1 cup flour
½ teaspoon salt
3 tablespoon sugar
¼ cup cocoa

½ cup shortening
1 teaspoon vanilla extract
Cold water

Sift the flour, salt, sugar, and cocoa together. Blend in the shortening with a pastry blender. Add the vanilla, and then just enough water to hold the mixture together. Roll out a board that is lightly floured or cocoaed. Place in an 8- or 9-inch pan, prick it all over with a fork.

Bake in a 400° F. oven for 8 minutes.

Makes 1 shell.

ORANGE PASTRY SHELL

1 cup flour	1 teaspoon grated orange
½ teaspoon salt	rind
½ cup shortening	Orange juice

1. Sift the flour and salt together. Cut in the shortening with a pastry blender. Add the orange rind. Add just enough orange juice to hold the mixture together. Chill.

2. Roll out the pastry and fit it into a 9-inch pie plate. Prick it all over with a fork. Bake in a 400° F. oven for 8 to 10 minutes.

Makes 1 shell.

TART SHELLS

The amount of pastry you make for a 2-crust pie can instead be used to make 8 to 10 tart shells. Use 3½-inch tart pans, or large muffin pans, turned upside down. Prick the pastry with a fork. Bake in a 450° F. oven for 10 to 12 minutes. Watch carefully, as they burn quickly. Cool before filling.

CHOCOLATE TARTS

Pastry for Chocolate Pastry Shell (pp. 251–252)	Chocolate Pastry Cream II (p. 97)
Seedless raspberry jam	Whipped cream

1. Make tart shells.

Bake them in a 400° F. oven for about 8 minutes. Cool.

2. Spread the shells with the jam and fill with the pastry cream. Top with whipped cream.

Makes 5 to 6 tarts.

Crumb and Other Crusts

CHOCOLATE GRAHAM-CRACKER CRUST

1 cup graham-cracker crumbs	2 ounces unsweetened chocolate (squares, melted, or envelopes)
¼ cup sugar	
¼ cup butter	1 teaspoon vanilla extract

Mix all the ingredients with a pastry blender and press into an 8- or 9-inch pie pan. Bake in a 375° F. oven for 8 minutes.

Makes 1 piecrust.

Variation: Add 2 or 3 teaspoons grated orange rind.

CHOCOLATE-WAFER CRUST

1½ cups chocolate-wafer crumbs (about 20 wafers)	1 tablespoon vanilla extract or other flavoring such as rum, or sherry
4 tablespoons soft butter	

Mix the ingredients and press into an 8- or 9-inch pie pan. Bake in a 375° F. oven for 8 minutes. Cool before filling.

Makes 1 piecrust.

Variation: VANILLA-WAFER CRUST

Use vanilla wafers instead of chocolate. This makes a delicious contrast for a chocolate filling.

NUT CRUMB CRUST

Use any kind of nuts for this. Vanilla wafers or chocolate wafers may be used for a delicious variation.

1 cup graham-cracker crumbs

½ cup walnuts, chopped or put through an electric blender

⅓ cup brown sugar

6 tablespoons soft butter

½ teaspoon vanilla extract

Mix the crumbs, nuts, and sugar. Blend in the butter with a pastry blender. Add the vanilla. Press the mixture into an 8- or 9-inch pie pan. Bake in a 275° F. oven for 8 to 10 minutes. Cool before filling.

COCONUT PIECRUST

This makes a deliciously different base for a chocolate cream pie.

2 tablespoons confectioners' sugar

1 tablespoon flour

2 cups grated coconut

3 tablespoons melted butter

Mix sugar and flour. Add coconut and mix. Blend in the melted butter. Pat into an 8- or 9-inch pie pan. Bake in a 350° F. oven for 8 to 10 minutes. Chill before filling.

Makes 1 piecrust.

FILBERT CRUST

1 egg white

¼ cup sugar

Pinch of salt

1½ cups filberts or hazelnuts, finely ground or put through an electric blender

1. Butter a 9-inch pie pan and line it with wax paper.

2. Beat the egg white until stiff. Add sugar slowly, and then the salt. When the meringue stands in peaks, fold in the ground nuts. Spread on the wax paper in the pie pan.

Bake in a 375° F oven for 10 minutes. Cool. Turn out, and carefully peel off the paper.

Cool the crust completely, then return it to the pan and fill with any chocolate pie filling.

Makes 1 piecrust.

SEMISWEET CHOCOLATE SHELL

A delicious double-chocolate flavor for chocolate pies, made in a foil pie pan.

2 cups semisweet chocolate bits	2 tablespoons butter or vegetable shortening
	2 tablespoons sugar

1. Melt the chocolate bits over hot water. Stir in the shortening and the sugar; blend. Spread on the bottom of a 9-inch foil pie pan. Chill.

2. Carefully turn out of the pan and fill with chocolate pie filling.

To serve, leave at room temperature for 30 minutes or so, for the pie shell is apt to chip if cut when too cold.

PIES AND FILLINGS

BLACK AND WHITE PIE

Crust

6 tablespoons butter
2 cups chocolate-wafer crumbs (25 to 30 wafers)

1 teaspoon vanilla extract

Melt the butter and mix with the crumbs. Add the vanilla. Press into a 10-inch pie plate. Bake in a 350° F. oven for 15 minutes. Cool.

Filling

3 eggs, separated
½ cup sugar
2 cups light cream
¼ teaspoon grated nutmeg

Pinch of salt
2 tablespoons dark rum
1 cup heavy cream
Grated semisweet chocolate

1. Beat the egg yolks until thick, add the sugar, and beat again. Stir in the light cream. Add the nutmeg, salt, and rum.

2. Whip the egg whites until they are stiff but not dry. Fold them into the egg-yolk mixture. Pour into the pie shell.

3. Bake in a 325° F. oven for about 24 minutes, or until the pie is firm. Cool.

4. Whip the heavy cream and spread on top. Sprinkle with grated semisweet chocolate.

Makes 6 to 8 servings.

BLACK BOTTOM PIE

For this old favorite, you may use either a baked pastry shell or a chocolate- or vanilla-wafer crust (p. 253). It will be a mouth-watering treat, creamy and richly chocolate-flavored.

9-inch baked pie shell
1 tablespoon unflavored gelatin
¼ cup cold water
4 egg yolks
¾ cup sugar
4 teaspoons cornstarch
Pinch of salt

2 cups rich milk (half-and-half is good)
3 ounces chocolate (squares, melted, or envelopes)
1 pint heavy cream, whipped
2 tablespoons dark rum
Grated semisweet chocolate

1. Bake the pie shell and cool it.

2. Soak the gelatin in the cold water.

3. Beat the egg yolks until very thick and light in color. Mix the sugar, cornstarch, and the salt and add. Beat well.

4. Put the milk and the 3 ounces of chocolate in a saucepan and stir over low heat until blended. Then stir this hot mixture slowly into the egg-yolk mixture, beating as you pour. Cook over hot water until the custard is smooth and thickens slightly. Add the gelatin and stir to dissolve. Set in the refrigerator till partially set.

5. When thickened, but not completely set, fold in half of the whipped cream, and the rum. Pour into the pie shell.

6. When set, top the pie with the rest of the whipped cream, and sprinkle the grated chocolate over the top.

Makes 6 to 8 servings.

CHEESECAKE PIE WITH CHOCOLATE

This may seem a bit complicated, but is well worth the effort involved.

Crust

1½ cups chocolate-wafer crumbs (about 20 wafers)	6 tablespoons soft butter
	1 teaspoon vanilla extract

Mix all together with a pastry blender. Press on the bottom of a 9-inch pie plate.

Filling

2 eggs	8 ounces soft cream cheese
¼ cup sugar	1 teaspoon vanilla extract
¼ cup honey	

1. Beat the eggs, add the sugar and honey, then the cheese. Blend well, add the vanilla, and spread on the crumb crust.

2. Bake in a 350° F. oven for 20 minutes.

Sauce

1 ounce chocolate (square or envelope)	¼ cup sugar
	Few grains of salt
3 tablespoons milk	1 teaspoon vanilla extract

1. Stir chocolate and milk together over low heat until blended.

2. Add the sugar and salt and cook for a few minutes until the sauce is thick and smooth. Cool slightly and add vanilla. Spread over the baked cream-cheese filling.

Topping

1½ cups sour cream	1 teaspoon vanilla extract
½ cup confectioners' sugar	

1. Add the sour cream to the sugar and beat for only 5 minutes. Longer beating will thin the cream. Add the vanilla.

2. Spread the topping over the chocolate layer and put the pie back in the oven for 5 minutes. Chill overnight.

Makes 6 to 8 servings.

ALMOND CHOCOLATE/MARSHMALLOW PIE

9-inch baked pie shell
3 ounces chocolate
(squares, cut up,
or envelopes)
¼ cup milk
Pinch of salt
32 large marshmallows,
cut up

1 tablespoon vanilla extract
1 teaspoon almond extract
1 cup heavy cream,
whipped
Almond halves, toasted

1. Bake and cool the pie shell.

2. Put chocolate, milk, salt, and marshmallows in a saucepan over low heat or in the top of a double boiler over hot water. Cook and stir until all ingredients are blended. Cool. Add vanilla and almond extracts. Fold in the whipped cream, and pour into the pie shell.

Arrange almond halves on top in a design.

Makes 6 to 8 servings.

CHOCOLATE BOURBON PIE

Pecan Pastry (p. 249)
1 cup semisweet chocolate
bits
1 ounce chocolate (square
or envelope)

2 eggs, separated
1 extra egg yolk
¼ cup bourbon
1 cup heavy cream,
whipped

1. Bake the pastry shell and cool it.

2. Combine both chocolates and melt over hot water. Cool slightly.

3. Beat egg yolks until thick and creamy. Slowly add the chocolate, beating as you pour.

4. Beat egg whites until stiff and fold them into the chocolate mixture. Then fold in the bourbon and the whipped cream. Pour into the baked and cooled crust. Chill.

Makes 6 servings.

Note: Any crumb crust (pp. 253–255) may be used with this filling.

CHOCOLATE CHIP PIE

Almond Pastry Shell (p. 251)	3 tablespoons flour
½ cup butter	½ cup chocolate chips
¼ cup sugar	Strawberry jam

1. Prepare the pastry and fit it into an 8-inch pie pan. Refrigerate while you make the filling.

2. Cream the butter and sugar together until light and creamy. Beat in the flour. Fold in the chocolate chips.

3. Spread strawberry jam over the pie shell. Pour the batter on top of this.

Bake in a 325° F. oven until golden brown, about 1 hour. Serve cold. Decorate with a wreath of whipped cream around the edge of the pie, and strawberry leaves around the plate.

Makes 6 servings.

CHOCOLATE CREAM-CHEESE PIE

9-inch Chocolate Pastry
Shell (pp. 251–252)
1 cup semisweet chocolate
bits
8 ounces cream cheese
¾ cup sugar

2 eggs, separated
Pinch of salt
1 cup heavy cream,
whipped
1 teaspoon vanilla extract
Chocolate shot

1. Bake and cool the pastry shell.

2. Melt the chocolate over hot water. Cool.

3. Cream the cheese and beat in ½ cup of the sugar. Add the egg yolks, one at a time, beating well after each addition.

4. Beat the egg whites until stiff, and add the remaining ¼ cup sugar gradually, then the salt, continuing to beat until peaks are formed.

5. Mix the chocolate into the cheese mixture. Fold in the meringue, then the whipped cream and vanilla. Pour the filling into the cooled pie shell, sprinkle chocolate shot on top, and chill well before serving.

Makes 6 to 8 servings.

CHOCOLATE FUDGE PIE

This is a very rich pie, bound to please all chocolate lovers.

10-inch baked pie shell
(p. 249)
2 cups milk
2 cups plus 6 tablespoons
sugar
2 ounces chocolate
(squares, cut up,
or envelopes)

¼ cup butter
3 eggs, separated
3 extra egg yolks
2 tablespoons flour
1 teaspoon vanilla extract
¼ teaspoon cream of tartar

1. Bake and cool the pie shell.

2. Combine the milk, 2 cups sugar, the chocolate, and butter.

Cook until the mixture reaches the soft-ball stage (238°). Cool slightly.

3. Beat all 6 egg yolks and the flour together. Stir the chocolate mixture slowly into this. Cook over hot water until thick. Cool slightly. Add the vanilla. Pour into the pie shell.

4. Whip the egg whites and cream of tartar until stiff. Add the 6 tablespoons sugar very slowly, and continue beating until stiff peaks are formed. Spread the meringue on the pie, covering the filling completely.

Bake in a 300° F. oven for 15 minutes, or until the meringue is slightly brown.

Makes 6 to 8 servings.

Variation: Make a MARSHMALLOW MERINGUE by using 3 egg whites, a few grains of salt, and ¾ cup marshmallow whip, omitting the cream of tartar and 6 tablespoons sugar.

CHOCOLATE PECAN PIE

This is the chocolate version of that delightfully rich Southern dessert, the pecan pie.

Pastry for a 1-crust pie (p. 249)	3 ounces chocolate (squares, melted, or envelopes)
4 eggs	
2 cups sugar	Pinch of salt
4 tablespoons melted butter	½ teaspoon lemon juice
	1 cup pecans

1. Make the pastry, roll it out, and use it to line a 9-inch pie pan.

2. Beat the eggs well, add the sugar, and continue to beat until light and creamy. Add the melted butter and the chocolate. Stir in the salt and lemon juice. Add the pecans and pour the filling into the unbaked pie shell.

Bake in a 375° F. oven for 30 minutes, or until set.

Serve warm with whipped cream.

Makes 8 servings.

CHOCOLATE RUM CREAM PIE

Crust

1½ cups chocolate-wafer crumbs (18 to 20 wafers)

4 tablespoons soft butter

2 tablespoons confectioners' sugar

1 tablespoon dark rum

Mix the ingredients well with a pastry blender and press into a 9-inch heatproof glass (or other) pie plate. Bake in a 350° F. oven for 8 to 10 minutes. Cool.

Filling

⅔ cup sugar

½ cup flour

Pinch of salt

3 eggs

½ cup dark rum

1½ cups milk

¼ cup currant jelly

½ teaspoon unflavored gelatin

1 cup heavy cream

Chocolate Leaves (p. 127)

1. Mix the sugar, flour, and salt.

2. Beat the eggs until thick and creamy. Add the dry ingredients, and then ¼ cup of the rum. Mix well.

3. Add the milk with the rest of the rum and heat. Stir slowly into the first mixture. Cook over hot water until the custard thickens, stirring all the while. Cool.

4. Stir the jelly over low heat until liquid. Spread over the cooled piecrust. Pour in the cold rum custard. Top with cream whipped with the gelatin. Decorate with Chocolate Leaves.

Makes 6 to 8 servings.

CHOCOLATE SHERRY CREAM PIE

10-inch baked pie shell
2 cups milk
2 ounces unsweetened
  chocolate (squares, cut
  up, or envelopes)
1 cup sugar
4 tablespoons flour
½ teaspoon salt
4 egg yolks

3 tablespoons butter
1 tablespoon vanilla ex-
  tract
1 tablespoon sherry
1 cup heavy cream,
  whipped
Chocolate Shavings
  (p. 126)

1. Bake and cool the pie shell.

2. Stir the milk and chocolate together in the top of a double boiler over hot water until blended.

3. Mix the sugar, flour, salt, and egg yolks. Beat well. Pour a little of the chocolate mixture onto the egg yolks, beating as you pour. Add the rest and return all to the double boiler. Cook, stirring, until thick. Add the butter. Cool. Stir in the vanilla and the sherry. Pour into the pie shell. Chill.

To serve, top with the whipped cream, and sprinkle chocolate shavings over the top.

Makes 6 to 8 servings.

GINGER FUDGE CREAM PIE

This may seem complicated, for it has a crust, a sauce, a filling, and a topping, but try it and you will be delighted.

Crust

1½ cups gingersnap
  crumbs (about
  18 cookies)

2 tablespoons sugar
4 tablespoons soft butter

Mix the ingredients well and press into a 9-inch heatproof glass (or other) pie plate. Bake in a 350° F. oven for 8 to 10 minutes. Cool.

Sauce

4 ounces chocolate
(squares, cut up,
or envelopes)

¼ cup sugar
⅓ cup water

Stir the ingredients over medium heat until the mixture is blended and smooth. Pour over the cooled crust, spreading evenly. Cool.

Filling

Custard Cream Filling
(p. 99)
1 cup heavy cream,
whipped

Chocolate Curls (p. 126)
Chopped candied ginger

Pour custard cream filling over the sauce. Top with the whipped cream. Make a wreath of Chocolate Curls around the edge and sprinkle chopped ginger in the center. Chill well before serving.

Makes 6 to 8 servings.

GRASSHOPPER PIE

Chocolate-Wafer Crust
(p. 253), 9 inches
1½ teaspoons unflavored
gelatin
⅓ cup light cream
4 egg yolks

¼ cup sugar
¼ cup crème de cacao
¼ cup green crème de
menthe
1 cup heavy cream

1. Make the chocolate-wafer crust. Cool.

2. Combine the gelatin and the light cream and allow to stand to soften the gelatin. Pour in the top of a double boiler and cook over hot water, stirring, until the gelatin is dissolved.

3. Beat the egg yolks well, and add the sugar gradually. Continue to beat until light and creamy. Stir in the liqueurs and then the gelatin and cream mixture.

4. Whip the heavy cream and fold it into the filling. Pour the filling into the prepared crust. Chill until firm.

To serve, decorate with Whipped-Cream Rosettes (p. 128) lightly flavored with either of the liqueurs used in the filling, and candied or fresh mint leaves.

Makes 6 to 8 servings.

NESSELRODE PIE

Crust

2 cups chocolate-wafer crumbs (25 to 30 wafers)	6 tablespoons butter
	1 teaspoon vanilla extract

Melt the butter and mix with the crumbs. Add the vanilla. Press into a 9-inch pie plate.

Bake in a 350° F. oven for 10 minutes. Cool.

Filling

3 eggs, separated	½ cup chopped candied fruits
1½ cups milk	
Pinch of salt	2 tablespoons dark rum
⅔ cup sugar	Semisweet Chocolate Curls (p. 126)
2 teaspoons gelatin	
1 tablespoon cold water	

1. Beat the egg yolks, milk, salt, and ⅓ cup of the sugar together in the top of a double boiler. Cook and stir over hot water until the mixture thickens.

2. Soak the gelatin in the water for a few minutes. Stir into the hot mixture until the gelatin is dissolved. Refrigerate until the custard begins to thicken.

3. Beat the egg whites until stiff. Beat in the remaining ⅓ cup sugar thoroughly. Fold this into the gelatin mixture. Add the fruits and the rum. Pour this into the cooled crumb crust and allow to set. Decorate with Chocolate Curls before serving.

Makes 6 to 8 servings.

ORANGE LIQUEUR PIE

9-inch Semisweet Chocolate Shell (p. 255)
1 tablespoon unflavored gelatin
¼ cup cold water
4 eggs, separated
8 tablespoons (½ cup) sugar
Pinch of salt

½ cup orange juice
1 tablespoon grated orange rind
2 tablespoons Curaçao
1 cup heavy cream, whipped
Chocolate Cutouts (p. 127)

1. Make the chocolate shell.

2. Soak the gelatin in the cold water.

3. Beat the egg yolks with 6 tablespoons of the sugar until thick and creamy. Add the salt, orange juice, and rind.

4. Cook over hot water, stirring, until thick and smooth. Add the gelatin and stir to dissolve. Cool slightly.

5. Whip the egg whites until stiff, and then beat in the remaining 2 tablespoons of sugar slowly. Fold this into the gelatin mixture. Add the Curaçao and pour the filling into the shell. Refrigerate until set.

To serve, top with the whipped cream and decorate with Chocolate Cut-outs.

Makes 6 to 8 servings.

PEPPERMINT CHOCOLATE PIE

This is a rich creamy pie, to which the bits of peppermint candy add a pleasant contrast.

9-inch Chocolate Pastry Shell (pp. 251–252)
1 cup butter
1½ cups confectioners' sugar
6 ounces chocolate (squares, melted, or envelopes)

1 tablespoon vanilla extract
4 eggs
½ cup crushed peppermint-stick candy
Whipped cream
Grated semisweet chocolate

1. Bake and cool the pastry shell.

2. Cream the butter and sugar well. Add the chocolate and the vanilla. Beat in the eggs, one at a time, beating well after each addition. Fold in the candy. Pour the filling into the pie shell. Chill.

When ready to serve, top with whipped cream and sprinkle with grated chocolate.

Makes 6 to 8 servings.

RUM GINGER PIE

This freezes well.

Crust

1½ cups gingersnap crumbs

½ cup soft butter
1 tablespoon dark rum

Blend the ingredients with a pastry blender. Press into a 9-inch pie pan. Bake in a 350° F. oven for 8 minutes. Cool.

1 tablespoon unflavored
gelatin
½ cup cold water
6 egg yolks, beaten
1 cup sugar

3 tablespoons chopped
crystalized ginger
2 cups heavy cream
½ cup dark rum
1 ounce semisweet Choco-
late Shavings (p. 126)

1. Soak the gelatin in the cold water. Stir over low heat until gelatin is dissolved.

2. Beat the egg yolks until thick and lemon-colored. Beat in the sugar gradually, then slowly add the gelatin and the ginger. Refrigerate until partially set.

3. Whip the cream; add the rum slowly. Fold half of the cream into the gelatin mixture. Pour into the crust. Top with the remaining whipped cream, and sprinkle the chocolate shavings on top.

Makes 6 to 8 servings.

SOUR-CREAM CHOCOLATE PIE

Use any pastry shell recipe that appeals to you. We like Pecan Pastry (p. 249) with this.

8-inch baked pastry shell
1 cup semisweet chocolate
bits
3 eggs, separated
2 tablespoons water

1 cup thick sour cream
Pinch of salt
⅓ cup honey
2 tablespoons dark rum
Grated semisweet chocolate

1. Bake and cool the pastry shell.

2. Melt the chocolate over hot water. Cool slightly.

3. Beat the egg yolks, add the water, and stir this slowly into the chocolate. Blend well. Fold in the sour cream.

4. Whip the egg whites and the salt until stiff. Add the honey slowly, continuing to beat until peaks are formed. Fold this into the rest of the filling. Add the rum. Pour into the cooled pastry shell. Decorate with grated semisweet chocolate. Chill.

Makes 6 to 8 servings.

SOUTHERN LIME PIE

A light delicious ending for a buffet supper or Sunday lunch.

9-inch Chocolate-Wafer
  Crust (p. 253)
½ pound marshmallows
⅓ cup light cream
2 tablespoons lime juice
1 teaspoon grated lime
  rind

Few drops of green food
  coloring
1 cup heavy cream,
  whipped
3 ounces semisweet choco-
  late, grated
Chocolate Curls (p. 126)

1. Bake and cool the piecrust.

2. Put marshmallows and cream in the top of a double boiler. Heat over hot water and stir to blend. Cool.

3. Add the lime juice and rind and the green coloring; chill until the filling is thick.

4. Fold in the whipped cream and the grated chocolate. Pour into the prepared and cooled crust. Refrigerate to set.

Top with additional whipped cream, if you like, and put a wreath of chocolate curls around the edge.

Makes 6 to 8 servings.

RASPBERRY ALMOND PIE

The rich nutty taste of the almonds blended with the raspberry jam makes an unusual delicious pie.

8-inch Chocolate-Wafer Crust (p. 253)	2 eggs
½ cup butter	½ cup ground almonds
½ cup sugar	1 cup seedless raspberry jam

1. Mix the crust and press it on the bottom of an 8-inch pie plate, but do not bake it. Set it in the refrigerator while preparing the filling.

2. Cream the butter and the sugar together. Add the eggs, one at a time, beating well after each addition. Stir in the ground almonds.

3. Remove the pie plate from the refrigerator. Carefully spread the jam on top of the crust. Pour the batter on top of this, spreading evenly.

Bake in a 350° F. oven for 30 minutes, or until the pie has become a delicate brown. Cool.

To serve: Arrange Whipped-Cream Rosettes (p. 128) around the edge of the pie.

Makes 6 to 8 servings.

CHOCOLATE
BEVERAGES

BRANDIED COCOA

3 tablespoons cocoa	½ cup boiling water
3 tablespoons sugar	1 quart milk
Pinch of salt	¼ cup brandy

Mix the cocoa, sugar, and salt in a saucepan. Add the boiling water and stir to mix. Add the milk and bring to the boiling point. Add the brandy and serve.

Makes about 8 servings.

Variation: MOCHA COCOA

Substitute strong coffee for the brandy and add ½ teaspoon vanilla extract.

CHOCOLATE ALMOND FLOAT

¼ cup blanched almonds	1 teaspoon sugar
1 cup warm water	¼ teaspoon almond extract
1 ounce semisweet choco- late	1 scoop of soft chocolate ice cream

1. Put the almonds and the water in an electric blender and blend until the nuts are as fine as possible.

2. Melt the chocolate over hot water, cool, and add to the almond milk with the sugar and almond extract. Blend.

3. Pour into a tall chilled glass. Add the ice cream and stir briefly.

Makes 1 serving.

CHOCOLATE EGGNOG

A wonderful cure for a midafternoon slump.

1 egg	¾ cup chilled milk
1 teaspoon sugar	Whipped cream
Few grains of salt	Grated nutmeg
2 teaspoons Chocolate	
Syrup (p. 205)	

1. Beat the egg well, then beat in the sugar, salt, and chocolate syrup. Add the milk and blend.

2. Pour into a tall chilled glass. Top with a spoonful of whipped cream and grate a little nutmeg on top.

Makes 1 serving.

CHOCOLATE MINT COOLER

Nothing so wonderful on a hot summer's day or, in fact, any time at all.

½ cup shaved ice	1 tablespoon crème de
2 tablespoons Chocolate	menthe
Syrup (p. 205)	Chocolate ice cream
½ cup extrastrong coffee, chilled	

1. Put the shaved ice in a tall chilled glass. Pour the syrup into the coffee and mix well. Pour over the ice. Add the crème de menthe and stir to blend.

2. Top with rather soft ice cream; you may use vanilla, but we find chocolate the most delicious. Stir slightly and sip through a straw.

Makes 1 serving.

CHOCOLATE MINT SHAKE

3 tablespoons Chocolate
   Syrup (p. 205)
1 cup chilled milk

1 scoop of peppermint ice
   cream

Shake the syrup and milk until blended or put in an electric blender for a few seconds. Add the ice cream and blend. Pour into a chilled glass and serve.

Makes 1 serving.

CHOCOLATE MOCHA FLOAT

½ cup Chocolate Syrup
   (p. 205)
2 cups cold strong coffee
2 cups cold milk

1 tablespoon dark rum
4 to 6 scoops of chocolate
   or coffee ice cream
Ground cinnamon

Blend syrup, coffee, milk, and rum thoroughly. Pour into chilled glasses. Top each with a scoop of ice cream and a dash of cinnamon.

Makes 4 to 6 servings.

CHOCOLATE ORANGE SODA

1 can (6 ounces) frozen
   orange juice
½ cup (more or less, ac-
   cording to your love for
   chocolate) chocolate or
   cocoa syrup

1 quart chocolate ice
   cream
1 quart cold carbonated
   water

1. Thaw the orange juice but do not dilute it. Blend it with the chocolate syrup and divide it among 8 glasses.

2. Add a scoop of ice cream to each. Pour in the carbonated water and stir.

Makes 8 sodas.

CHOCOLATE SUNDAE COOLER

A delightful drink on a warm summer day.

½ cup Chocolate Syrup (p. 205)
1 teaspoon instant coffee powder
Few grains of salt
⅓ cup sherry
1 cup cold milk
½ pint vanilla ice cream
Grated nutmeg

Put all ingredients in an electric blender. Blend briefly at high speed. Pour into 4 chilled glasses and grate a little nutmeg on the top.

Makes 4 servings.

CINNAMON CHOCOLATE FRAPPÉ

Serve this to guests old or young; they will love it.

1 cup Chocolate Syrup (p. 205)
6 cups chilled milk
1 quart soft cinnamon ice cream

Blend the syrup and the milk. Add the ice cream and stir. Spoon into tall chilled glasses.

Serve immediately.

Makes 8 to 10 servings.

COCOA MEXICAN STYLE

1 teaspoon cocoa
2 teaspoons sugar
1 teaspoon ground toasted almonds

¼ cup water
¾ cup milk
2 drops of almond extract

Put all the ingredients except the almond extract in a saucepan and simmer for 3 minutes. Add the almond extract and serve.

Makes one 1-cup serving.

FRENCH CHOCOLATE

1 ounce unsweetened chocolate (square or envelope)
½ cup water
6 tablespoons sugar

Few grains of salt
¼ cup heavy cream, whipped
2 cups hot milk

1. Put chocolate, water, sugar, and salt in a saucepan, and stir over low heat until well blended. Cook for 10 minutes, stirring so that the mixture does not scorch.

2. Cool. Fold in the whipped cream.

To serve, pour the hot milk into cups, and top each cup with some of the chocolate cream.

Makes 3 servings.

FROSTED CHOCOLATE

3 tablespoons Chocolate Syrup (p. 205)
1 cup milk

2 tablespoons crème de cacao
2 scoops of soft chocolate ice cream
Grated nutmeg

Put the syrup, milk, and crème de cacao in a bowl and mix well. Add the ice cream and beat till smooth and creamy. Pour into a large chilled glass, and grate a little nutmeg on the top.

Makes 1 serving.

MOCHA CHOCOLATE

1½ ounces unsweetened chocolate (squares, melted, or envelopes)
¼ cup sugar
Pinch of salt
1 cup boiling water

1 cup milk
1 cup cream
1 teaspoon instant coffee powder
½ teaspoon vanilla extract

Put the chocolate, sugar, salt, and water in a saucepan and stir over low heat until blended. Then add the milk and cream, and bring to a boil. Add the coffee powder and stir to dissolve. Whisk to a froth, add the vanilla, and serve.

Makes about 4 servings.

MOCHA MILKSHAKE

¼ cup Chocolate Syrup (p. 205)
1 tablespoon instant coffee powder

2 teaspoons honey
2 scoops of chocolate ice cream
1½ cups rich milk

Put syrup, coffee powder, honey, and ice cream in an electric blender. Turn on high until blended. Gradually pour in the milk. Serve in chilled glasses.

Makes 2 servings.

MOCHA NECTAR

In South America, they discovered long ago that chocolate and coffee flavors make a happy combination.

½ cup shaved ice
½ cup cold strong coffee
2 tablespoons Chocolate Syrup (p. 205)

½ teaspoon vanilla extract
Whipped cream

Put the ice in a tall, chilled glass. Stir the coffee, chocolate syrup, and vanilla together to blend. Pour over the ice. Stir well and top with whipped cream.

Makes 1 serving.

RICH COCOA

Serve this steaming hot on a cold winter's day; or chill, and serve in cold glasses on a summer afternoon.

3 tablespoons cocoa
4 tablespoons sugar
Few grains of salt
½ cup water

4 cups rich milk
Few drops of vanilla extract

Mix cocoa, sugar, and salt. Add water and simmer for 2 to 3 minutes. Add milk and vanilla, beat until frothy, and serve.

Makes 6 servings.

CANDY AND CONFECTIONS

*T*HE MAKING OF CANDY in the home is not as common as it used to be when our grandmothers, as little girls, whiled away a long Sunday afternoon by pulling taffy or popping corn for popcorn balls, but school girls still go home and stir up a batch of fudge, and a gift of homemade goodies is gratefully received at any time.

Most of the recipes included are simple ones for those who wish to leave the more difficult ones to the professional. However, here is some general information to guide you.

An experienced candy maker can judge when the soft- or firm-ball stage is reached by dropping a bit into a cup of cold water, and is able to tell, by the length of the thread dropped from a spoon, what stage has been reached by the cooking syrup. For most of us, the candy thermometer is the answer; here is a chart to go by:

STAGE	TEMPERATURE ON CANDY THERMOMETER
Thread	230° to 234° F.
Soft ball	234° to 238° F.
Firm ball	244° to 248° F.
Hard ball	248° to 254° F.
Very hard ball	254° to 260° F.
Light crack	270° to 285° F.
Hard crack	290° to 300° F.
Carmelized sugar	310° to 338° F.

Stir candy only until the sugar is dissolved and the boiling point has been reached. Stirring after this results in a sugary product. The use of corn syrup is a help in this respect.

Candy containing chocolate, butter, cream, and molasses burns easily, so keep the heat low.

Allow a candy mixture to cool before beating it to achieve a creamy product.

Add butter after removing from the heat, and vanilla when the mixture has cooled.

CHOCOLATE FOR DIPPING

You probably will not find dipping chocolate such as is used by professional candy makers on your grocer's shelf, but you can make a mixture that will do very well.

You may use semisweet chocolate, or half milk chocolate and half unsweetened chocolate.

Melt the chocolate over hot, not boiling, water. Cook until a candy thermometer reads 130° F., then cool to 85° F. This is the proper temperature for dipping and should be maintained throughout the time you are dipping.

CHOCOLATE NUTS. Use Chocolate for Dipping (p. 285). Dip whole nuts into the chocolate, then allow them to harden on wax paper.

CHOCOLATE CANDIED PEELS. Dip candied orange peel, glacéed pineapple wedges, or glacéed cherries into the Chocolate for Dipping (p. 285). Let the pieces harden on wax paper.

BRANDIED CHOCOLATE CHERRIES. Buy brandied Bing cherries or make your own. Drain them well. Melt Chocolate for Dipping (p. 285) and, holding a cherry by the stem, turn each one in the chocolate until well coated. Dry on wax paper.

BUTTER NUT BRITTLE

A delicious easy-to-make confection.

1 cup sugar	1½ cups broken pecan
Pinch of salt	meats
¼ cup water	2 cups semisweet chocolate
½ cup butter	bits, melted

1. Butter a cooky sheet.

2. Combine the sugar, salt, water, and butter in a saucepan, and cook to the light-crack stage (285° F. on a candy thermometer). Add ½ cup of the nut meats. Pour onto the center of the prepared cooky sheet. Cool.

3. Cover with half of the melted chocolate. When the chocolate is firm, turn the candy over and cover the other side with the rest of the chocolate. Spread the remaining nuts evenly over the top.

4. When cold, break up into pieces. Store in an airtight box, with wax paper between layers.

Makes about 1 pound.

CHOCOLATE ALMOND BARK

1 cup sugar
3 ounces chocolate
(squares, melted,
or envelopes)

1 teaspoon vanilla extract
1 cup toasted slivered
blanched almonds

1. Place the sugar in a heavy skillet and stir over low heat until melted. Add the chocolate and the vanilla and blend. Add the almonds, and stir to mix quickly. Pour on a cooky sheet covered with wax paper and spread evenly. Cool.

Break into pieces and store in an airtight box.

Makes about ¾ pound.

CHOCOLATE ALMOND TRUFFLES

1 ounce chocolate (square,
cut up, or envelope)
8 ounces semisweet choco-
late, cut up
¾ cup undiluted evapo-
rated milk

Few grains of salt
1 teaspoon brandy
Finely ground toasted al-
monds

1. Cook both kinds of chocolate, evaporated milk, and salt in the top of a double boiler over boiling water for 15 minutes. Cool. Add brandy and stir to mix.

2. Form into balls and roll in chopped almonds.

Makes about ½ pound.

CHOCOLATE CARAMELS

A favorite confection which melts in the mouth.

2 cups sugar
1 cup light corn syrup
¼ teaspoon salt
3 cups heavy cream
2 tablespoons butter

4 ounces chocolate
(squares, melted,
or envelopes)
1 tablespoon vanilla extract

1. Mix the sugar, syrup, salt, and 1 cup of the cream in a saucepan, and bring to a boil over medium heat. Boil, covered, for 5 minutes. Turn heat down and cook, stirring frequently, until the mixture forms a soft ball (234° F. on a candy thermometer). Continue to cook and stir as you add the rest of the cream and the butter very slowly; do not allow the candy to stop boiling. When all the cream and butter are incorporated, remove from the heat.

2. Quickly stir in the chocolate and the vanilla. When blended, pour into a buttered 8-inch pan. Cool overnight.

3. Invert pan, turning out the candy. Cut into squares, using a sharp knife with a sawing motion. Wrap each caramel separately.

Makes about 4 dozen caramels.

CHOCOLATE COCONUT SQUARES

2 cups sugar
½ cup water
4 tablespoons corn syrup
3 ounces chocolate
(squares, melted,
or envelopes)

2 cups grated coconut
1 teaspoon vanilla extract
1 tablespoon butter

1. Butter an 8-inch-square pan.

2. Combine the sugar, water, corn syrup, and chocolate in a saucepan and bring to boil over medium heat. Boil for 5 minutes.

Turn heat down and cook, stirring frequently, until it reaches the soft-ball stage (236° F. on a candy thermometer). Cool to lukewarm. Stir in the coconut. Add the vanilla and butter and beat until thick and creamy. Pour into the buttered pan. When cold, cut into squares.

Makes about 1½ pounds.

CHOCOLATE DIVINITY

Divinity has long been a favorite confection. It is smooth and light, and this chocolate version is one of the best.

2 cups sugar	3 ounces chocolate
⅔ cup water	(squares, melted and
½ cup light corn syrup	cooled, or envelopes)
¼ teaspoon salt	1 tablespoon vanilla ex-
3 egg whites	tract
	¾ cup broken walnut meats

1. Butter a cooky sheet.

2. Mix the sugar, water, corn syrup, and salt in a saucepan. Stir until the mixture comes to a boil. Cover and simmer for 5 minutes. Remove cover and continue cooking until the hard-ball stage is reached (252° F. on a candy thermometer). As the syrup cooks, brush sugar crystals up occasionally from the sides of the pan with a damp pastry brush or a stick wrapped in damp cheesecloth.

3. Meanwhile, whip the egg whites until they are stiff. When the syrup is ready, pour it very slowly onto the beaten whites, then beat until peaks are formed (30 to 35 minutes). Stir in the cooled chocolate and the vanilla. Fold in the nut meats.

4. Drop from a teaspoon onto the buttered cooky sheet. When set, store in an airtight box.

Makes 3½ to 4 dozen pieces.

CHOCOLATE FONDANT

4 ounces chocolate (squares, cut up, or envelopes)	1½ cups water
	¼ teaspoon cream of tartar
3 cups sugar	1 teaspoon vanilla extract

1. Put chocolate, sugar, water, and cream of tartar in a saucepan. Stir over low heat until sugar is dissolved. Bring to a boil. Boil, covered, for 5 minutes. Uncover, and cook without stirring. Remove crystals forming on the side of the pan, being careful not to allow them to drop into the syrup. Cook to the soft-ball stage (238° F. on a candy thermometer).

2. Pour the candy onto a damp platter, or, if you are fortunate enough to have a marble slab, use that. Allow the candy to cool to about 100° F. Work the fondant with a metal spatula until it is creamy. Put it in a bowl, cover it, and allow it to rest for an hour or so.

3. Knead the fondant until it is soft and smooth. Put it back into the bowl, cover it with a slightly damp towel, put wax paper over the towel, and let ripen for 24 hours. Shape into candies. This can be melted and used to ice *Petits Fours* (see pp. 107–108).

Variations: FONDANT

2½ cups sugar	2 tablespoons butter
1 cup milk	⅛ teaspoon cream of tartar

Follow the directions for Chocolate Fondant, using these ingredients to replace those in recipe.

OLD-FASHIONED CHOCOLATE DROPS

Shape Fondant (above) into small mounds and dip into Chocolate for Dipping (p. 285). Place on wax paper until set.

PEPPERMINT CREAMS

Add ¼ teaspoon peppermint extract to the above fondant, and, if you wish, a little red coloring.

Shape into flat patties and top with melted chocolate. Use Chocolate for Dipping (p. 285).

CHOCOLATE FRUIT ROUNDS

An uncooked confection that combines fruit flavors with that of chocolate.

½ cup almonds	Grated rind of 1 orange
½ cup pecan meats	1 teaspoon almond extract
½ cup dates	Confectioners' sugar
½ cup figs	1 ounce chocolate, melted
1 tablespoon orange juice	Almond halves

1. Grind the nuts and the fruits. Mix in the orange juice and rind, and the almond extract. Shape into balls and roll in confectioners' sugar.

2. Flatten the balls slightly, brush with the melted chocolate, and press an almond half of top of each. Store in an airtight box between layers of wax paper.

Makes about ¾ pound.

CHOCOLATE NOUGAT DROPS

1 tablespoon honey	1 teaspoon vanilla extract
1 cup confectioners' sugar	1 teaspoon almond extract
Few grains of salt	Chocolate for Dipping
1 cup chopped almonds	(p. 285)

1. Butter a large platter.

2. Stir honey and sugar over low heat until the sugar is dissolved and blended with the honey. Add the salt and the almonds. Stir over low heat until the candy becomes golden. Add the flavorings. Drop by spoonfuls onto the buttered platter. Allow to cool.

3. Make Chocolate for Dipping. Drop each mound of nougat into the chocolate and place on wax paper t set.

Makes about ½ pound.

CHOCOLATE NUT CREAMS

This is rather like divinity with a chocolate touch.

3½ cups sugar
¾ cup corn syrup
1½ cups water
3 egg whites

2 teaspoons vanilla extract
1½ cups walnuts, broken
coarsely
2 ounces chocolate, melted

1. Boil the sugar, corn syrup, and water until it reaches the hard-ball stage (254° F. on a candy thermometer).

2. Beat the egg whites until stiff, and pour the syrup slowly over them, beating as you pour. Continue to beat until thick and creamy. Stir in the vanilla and nuts, and pour into a buttered 9-inch-square pan. Cool. Turn out onto wax paper, spread with the melted chocolate, and cut into squares.

Makes 81 squares.

CHOCOLATE NUT CRUNCH

1 cup sugar
Few grains of salt
3 ounces chocolate
(squares, melted,
or envelopes)

1 cup chopped toasted
blanched almonds

1. Butter a pan or put out a sheet of wax paper.

2. In a heavy skillet stir the sugar and salt over low heat until the sugar is carmelized. Add the chocolate, stir quickly, and then fold in the nuts. Mix well. Spoon onto the paper or into the pan, flattening each bit out as you go. Cool.

Makes about ¾ pound.

CHOCOLATE PECAN ROUNDS

2 cups sugar
1¼ cups water
2 tablespoons corn syrup
1 teaspoon vanilla extract

3 ounces chocolate
(squares, melted,
or envelopes)
Cocoa
Pecan halves

1. Bring sugar, water, and corn syrup to a boil, stirring as the mixture cooks. Continue to simmer without stirring until a soft ball is formed (238° F. on a candy thermometer). Cool to about 110° F.

2. Pour onto a table top or marble slab and turn over with a spatula until the candy is creamy. Add the vanilla and chocolate, a little at a time, working each bit in after it is added. Knead to blend. Place in a plastic bag and store in the refrigerator for 2 or 3 days.

3. Shape fondant into small balls, roll in cocoa, and press a pecan half on each one.

Makes about 1 pound.

CHOCO-MALLOW FUDGE

1⅔ cups sugar
Pinch of salt
⅔ cup light cream
1½ cups semisweet choco-
late bits

2 cups small marshmallows
1 teaspoon vanilla extract
½ cup walnuts, coarsely
chopped

1. Butter an 8-inch-square pan.

2. Stir sugar, salt, cream, and chocolate bits over low heat. Stir until the mixture comes to a boil. Simmer for a few minutes, or until chocolate is melted and all ingredients are blended.

3. Remove from heat. Add marshmallows, vanilla, and nuts. Beat until marshmallows are melted. Pour into prepared pan. Mark into squares. Cool. Cut into squares.

Makes 3 dozen pieces.

CHOCOLATE PECAN TOFFEE

This is a "can't fail" candy. The brown sugar and the pecans are a delicious combination.

¾ cup firmly packed brown sugar
½ cup butter

½ cup pecan meats, finely ground, or put through an electric blender
1 teaspoon vanilla extract
½ cup semisweet chocolate bits

1. Butter an 8-inch-square cake pan.

2. Mix the sugar and butter in a saucepan and bring it to a boil over low heat, stirring so that it will not scorch, until it reaches 270° F. on a candy thermometer. This will take about 7 minutes. Quickly add the nuts and vanilla, and spread on the prepared pan. Sprinkle with the chocolate bits, spreading the chocolate as it melts over the hot candy. Cool. Break into pieces.

Store in an airtight container, with wax paper between layers.

Makes about ¾ pound.

CHRISTMAS FUDGE

1 cup milk
2 cups sugar
4 tablespoons corn syrup
2 ounces chocolate (squares, cut up, or envelopes)

2 teaspoons vanilla extract
1 teaspoon almond extract
1 cup candied cherries, halved
1 cup chopped toasted blanched almonds

1. Mix the milk, sugar, corn syrup, and chocolate. Bring to a boil, stirring, and continue to cook without stirring until the mixture reaches the soft-ball stage (238° F. on a candy thermometer). Cool to about 110° F.

2. Add the vanilla and almond extracts. Beat until thick. Stir in the cherries and almonds, and pour into a buttered 9-inch pan. When set, cut into squares.

Makes about 81 squares.

Variation: Use mixed glacéed fruits such as you use for fruitcake instead of the cherries and almonds.

ENGLISH TOFFEE

Deliciously buttery, packed with nuts, and chocolate covered.

1 cup butter	1 cup walnut meats, put through an electric blender or finely chopped
1 cup sugar	
3 tablespoons water	
¼ teaspoon salt	
	1 tablespoon vanilla extract
	6 ounces (squares) semisweet chocolate, grated

1. Butter a 9-inch-square cake pan.

2. Melt the butter and add the sugar, water, and salt. Bring to a boil and cook, watching so that it will not burn, to the hard-crack stage (300° F. on a candy thermometer). Remove from stove and add ¾ of the nuts and the vanilla. Pour into the buttered pan.

Sprinkle the grated chocolate over the hot toffee and spread quickly. Sprinkle the remaining nuts on top. Allow to harden.

3. When the candy is hard, turn out and break up into uneven pieces. Store in an airtight box, putting foil or wax paper between layers.

Makes about 1½ pounds.

HONEY CARAMELS

5 ounces chocolate (squares, melted, or envelopes)	2 cups sugar
	¼ teaspoon salt
	2 cups heavy cream
1 cup plus 2 tablespoons corn syrup	2 tablespoons butter
¼ cup honey	1 tablespoon vanilla extract

1. Butter an 8-inch-square pan.

2. Mix chocolate, corn syrup, honey, sugar, salt, and 1 cup of the cream in a saucepan. Bring to a boil. Cook, stirring, to 244° F. on a candy thermometer, or the firm-ball stage. Add the second cup of cream and the butter and continue to cook until 242° F. is reached. Add the vanilla and pour into prepared pan.

When cold, cut into squares and wrap.

Makes 64 caramels.

MARSHMALLOW NUT CREAMS

4 tablespoons cocoa	24 small marshmallows
2 cups sugar	1 cup Brazil nuts, coarsely chopped
1 cup milk	
4 tablespoons butter	1 teaspoon vanilla extract

1. Mix the cocoa and sugar. Add the milk and butter, and cook to the soft-ball stage (238° F. on a candy thermometer). Add the marshmallows to the hot candy, fold them in, and then fold in the nuts. Add the vanilla, stir to mix, and pour the candy into a buttered 8-inch-square pan. Cool. Cut into squares.

Makes 64 squares.

MARZIPAN POTATOES

Marzipan is a very elegant confection and surprisingly simple to make. The potato shape is a traditional one.

1 cup Almond Paste (below)
1 cup confectioners' sugar
Few drops of rosewater
Cocoa and sifted confectioners' sugar, mixed
Bits of slivered almond

1. Mix the almond paste, sugar, and rosewater thoroughly. Knead on a marble slab or a platter for 15 to 20 minutes. Form into small potatoes. Roll in the mixture of cocoa and sugar. Stud with bits of almond to represent the eyes of the potato.

ALMOND PASTE

BLENDER METHOD

½ cup orange juice
2 cups almonds, blanched
1 cup sugar

1. Put the orange juice in an electric blender, add 1 cup of the almonds, and blend until nuts are chopped fine. Add sugar and blend again. Add the second cup of almonds and blend until all is very fine and smooth. Refrigerate until ready to use.

Makes about 3 cups.

GRINDER METHOD

1 pound almonds, blanched (2⅔ cups)
1 pound granulated sugar (2 cups)
1 cup water
½ cup orange juice
Confectioners' sugar, sifted

1. Grind the nuts several times in a food grinder, using the finest blade.

2. Mix granulated sugar and water in a saucepan and cook to 240° F. on a candy thermometer. Add the ground nuts and the orange juice. Stir until creamy.

Candy and Confections ◆ 297

3. Dust a marble slab or large platter with confectioners' sugar. Transfer the paste to this and let it cool. Store in an airtight box for a week before using.

Makes about 3 to 4 cups.

NUT CLUSTERS

An everyday favorite, easy to make. I use salted mixed nuts, but you can use any kind you like, salted or unsalted.

1 ounce chocolate (square, cut up, or envelope)	1½ cups nuts
½ cup semisweet chocolate bits	Pinch of salt if nuts are unsalted
1 tablespoon butter	1 tablespoon vanilla extract

1. Melt both kinds of chocolate together over hot water. Stir in the butter, nuts, and vanilla. Drop by spoonfuls onto wax paper. Cool. Store in an airtight box with wax paper between the layers.

Makes 2 to 3 dozen clusters.

OLD-FASHIONED FUDGE

Once you have tried this recipe, you will never use another.

3 cups sugar	4 ounces chocolate (squares, melted, or envelopes)
1 tablespoon unflavored gelatin	
½ cup corn syrup	1 tablespoon vanilla extract
1 cup milk	
1 cup butter	1 cup broken walnut meats

1. Butter a cake pan (7 x 9 inches) or one of similar size.

2. Mix sugar, gelatin, corn syrup, milk, butter, and chocolate in a saucepan. Stir over low heat until the mixture reaches the soft-ball stage (238° F. on a candy thermometer). Remove from the stove and allow to cool to lukewarm (110° F.).

3. Add vanilla and beat until the candy has lost its sheen. Mix in the nuts quickly and turn all into the prepared pan. When firm, cut into squares.

This fudge takes a little while to set. I usually leave it overnight in the refrigerator.

Makes 63 squares.

PEANUT CRUNCH

2¼ cups sugar
1¼ cups butter
½ cup water
1 tablespoon vinegar
1 teaspoon salt
2 cups peanuts, put through an electric blender

1 teaspoon baking soda
1 tablespoon vanilla extract
1 cup semisweet chocolate bits, melted

1. Butter a 9-inch-square pan.

2. Put sugar, butter, water, vinegar, and salt in a saucepan. Bring to a boil, and cook until the mixture reaches the light-crack stage (285° F. on a candy thermometer). Stir in 1 cup of the peanuts mixed with the baking soda. Add the vanilla. When well mixed, pour into the buttered pan and cool.

3. Spread with the melted chocolate and sprinkle the rest of the peanuts on top. When candy is set, break into pieces.

Store in an airtight box with foil or wax paper between layers.

Makes about 2 pounds.

PINEAPPLE FUDGE

3 ounces chocolate
(squares or envelopes)
¾ cup rich milk
2 cups sugar
Pinch of salt
4 tablespoons butter

1 tablespoon vanilla extract
½ cup candied pineapple,
cut up
⅔ cup chopped walnuts

1. Butter a pan, glass dish, or baking dish, about 8 inches square or one of similar size.

2. Put chocolate and milk in a saucepan and stir over low heat until well blended. Add sugar and salt. Simmer without stirring until the fudge reaches 234° F. on a candy thermometer (the soft-ball stage). Add the butter. Cool. Add the vanilla. When luke warm (110° F.), beat the fudge until it loses its gloss. Mix in the fruit and nuts quickly, and turn immediately into the buttered dish. Mark into squares. Cut when cold.

Makes 64 squares.

RUM CONFECTIONS

4 ounces chocolate
(squares, melted,
or envelopes)
2 tablespoons butter

1½ cups confectioners' sugar
2 egg yolks
1 tablespoon dark rum
Cocoa

1. Mix the chocolate, butter, and sugar in the top of a double boiler Stir over hot water until well blended. Cool slightly.

2. Beat egg yolks until thick and lemon-colored. Add the hot mixture slowly, beating as you add. Pour in the rum. Cool.

3. When stiff enough to handle, form into small balls, and roll in cocoa.

Makes 1 dozen.

SOUR-CREAM WALNUT FUDGE

I don't know whether the sour cream or the kneading is responsible for the velvety texture of this confection.

3 ounces chocolate
  (squares, melted,
  or envelopes)
2 cups sugar

⅔ cup sour cream
Pinch of salt
2 teaspoons vanilla extract
Walnut halves

1. Combine the chocolate, sugar, sour cream, and salt. Cook, stirring, until the mixture comes to a boil. Continue to cook over low heat without stirring until it reaches the soft-ball stage (234° F. on a candy thermometer). Add the vanilla.

2. Pour the candy onto a marble slab, if you have one, or your kitchen counter, or any similar flat surface. Allow the fudge to cool, and then work it with a spatula as you would fondant. When thick enough to handle, knead it, and pat it out on a buttered platter to the desired thickness. Cut into squares. Top each square with a walnut half.

Makes about 1¼ pounds.

FIX THAT MIX WITH CHOCOLATE

*T*ODAY IT SEEMS that everything is rush-rush-rush. No longer is a woman a mother and a homemaker alone. She is a chauffeur, a gardener, a P.-T.A. member, a member of the board of charitable organizations, a worker on drives to raise money for all sorts of worthy causes, or she may be a wage earner. The day of the double paycheck is here to stay.

A woman wishes, in spite of all this, to serve her family nutritious and delicious meals—meals attractive to the eye and appealing to the palate. To accomplish this miracle, there are times when a short cut is a blessing; a convenience food, a necessity.

For these occasions, I give you a few dishes in which the quality of the dish does not suffer, but the time spent in the kitchen is reduced to a matter of minutes. They should assist the bride, the busy mother of young children, the career girl, as well as the lazy gourmet to keep up her reputation as a cook and to also keep her family and friends happy, eagerly awaiting an invitation to dinner.

BROWNIE PUDDING CAKE

This looks and tastes like a fussy dessert, but can be done in a flash.

¾ cup firmly packed brown sugar
4 tablespoons Dutch cocoa
1 teaspoon vanilla extract

1½ cups boiling water
1 package (16 ounces) brownie mix

1. Mix sugar, cocoa, vanilla, and water in a buttered 9-inch-square cake pan.

2. Follow the directions on the box for cake brownies. Pour the batter into the pan on top of the cocoa mixture.

Bake in a 350° F. oven for about 35 minutes, or until the cake is springy to the touch. Turn out on a serving platter. The sauce is now on top of the cake.

Serve warm with ice cream.

Makes about 9 servings.

CHOCOLATE BROWNIE PIE

This is the same idea as a shoofly pie—a cake batter baked in a pastry shell.

1 baked pie shell
1 package (10 ounces) brownie mix

1 teaspoon vanilla extract
Whipped cream or ice cream

1. Make a pastry shell in a 10-inch pie pan.

2. Stir up the brownie mix according to the directions on the package. Add the vanilla. Pour into the pastry shell.

Bake in a 350° F. oven for 40 minutes, or until the center is springy to the touch. Cool. Serve with ice cream, or whipped cream.

Makes 6 to 8 servings.

CHOKALU BROWNIES

This is a real blessing for the cook in a hurry.

1 package (16 ounces) brownie mix
1 tablespoon Dutch cocoa
1 teaspoon vanilla extract

Coffee, cinnamon, or peppermint ice cream
Chokalu liqueur

1. Make the brownies following the directions on the box, but add the extra cocoa and the vanilla when mixing the batter.

To serve: Cut the brownies into squares, top each square with a scoop of ice cream, and pour the liqueur over all.

Makes 8 or 9 servings.

PEPPERMINT BROWNIE SANDWICHES

Make this from a mix, or use your favorite brownie recipe.

1 package (about 1 pound) brownie mix
2 tablespoons cocoa

1 teaspoon vanilla extract
Peppermint   Buttercream (p. 120)

1. Prepare two 8-inch-square pans as directed on the package of mix.

2. Make the brownies according to directions, but add the cocoa to the dry ingredients and stir in the vanilla with the liquid. Spread the batter thinly in the 2 pans.

Bake according to directions on the package, but remember that thin brownies will take less time to bake. Cool and remove from pans. Put together with Peppermint Buttercream and cut into bars.

Makes 32 sandwiches.

ANGEL TORTE WITH HAZELNUTS

A delicate chocolate nut dessert, nice to serve on special occasions.

1 package (about 1 pound) angel-food mix

2 ounces chocolate, (squares, melted, or envelopes)

1 tablespoon cognac

1½ cups hazelnuts, finely ground or put through an electric blender

Chocolate Buttercream Icing (p. 106)

1. Prepare the cake mix according to directions on the box, gently folding in the chocolate and cognac before adding the flour. Fold in 1¼ cups of the nuts, saving ¼ cup for the top. Pour into an unbuttered angel-cake pan.

2. Bake according to directions on the box. Cool.

3. Turn out of the pan and slice into 3 layers. Spread Chocolate Buttercream Icing on the layers, the top, and the sides. Sprinkle the top with the reserved ¼ cup of nuts.

Makes 8 to 10 servings.

CHOCOLATE FUDGE NUT CAKE

This is an upside-down version of a cake mix that will please you.

4 tablespoons brown sugar

¾ cup corn syrup

4 tablespoons butter

Pinch of salt

½ cup semisweet chocolate bits

1 package (about 1 pound) chocolate cake mix

1 egg

1 tablespoon vanilla extract

¾ cup water

1. Mix the brown sugar, corn syrup, butter, and salt in a saucepan. Stir over low heat until the mixture comes to a boil and is blended. Pour into a 9-inch-square cake pan. Set aside to cool. Sprinkle the chocolate bits on top.

2. Mix the cake batter according to the directions on the box, using ¾ cup water, the egg, and the vanilla. Pour this over the mixture in the pan.

Bake in a 350° F. oven for 35 to 40 minutes, or until the center is springy to the touch. Turn out on a serving plate.

Serve warm, topped with ice cream.

Makes **8** to **10** servings.

CHOCOLATE IN MAIN DISHES

*A*LTHOUGH IT MAY COME as a shock to many readers, chocolate is often used to embellish main dishes—poultry and meat dishes, that is—in many parts of the world. The festive dinners one often reads about were perhaps made memorable by the use of chocolate as an ingredient in the savory sauces that blend so well with meats and other ingredients. This is particularly true in the Latin American countries, as our recipes will demonstrate.

The flavor is not overpoweringly chocolatey in these dishes, as some cooks and diners may fear. Rather, it is an elusive, rich, savory fragrance and taste which nine out of ten diners will probably fail to identify with chocolate. Everyone seems to appreciate this "mystery ingredient," although if they were asked beforehand if they would enjoy it they would probably demur. No one ever forgets the unusual, palate-tickling taste.

The recipes include one for Turkey with Mole Sauce. This blends chocolate with various spices, tomatoes, and seasonings. Three chicken dishes are offered, one of which uses fruit most effectively, while the other dishes are more conventional—except for the chocolate used in creating them. Perhaps the most unusual recipe of the group is the Mexican Kidney-Bean Casserole in which the cooked poultry base is layered with beans and made memorable by the sauce (with its chocolate ingredient) poured over the layers.

None of the recipes is formidably difficult or time-consuming. The busy cook can accomplish all the other tasks concerned with getting a good dinner without undue strain. The cook, of course, will be buoyed up by the knowledge that her "mystery ingredient" will insure the complete success of the dinner party.

MEXICAN KIDNEY-BEAN CASSEROLE

This is a distant relation to that classic French dish cassoulet.

2 cans (1 pound, 4 ounces each) white kidney beans
2 cups diced cooked chicken or turkey
¼ cup tomato sauce
½ cup dry red wine
½ cup chopped onion
1 teaspoon salt
1 small garlic clove
½ ounce grated chocolate
Bread crumbs
Butter

1. Drain the beans, reserving ½ cup of the liquid. Add the tomato sauce, wine, onion, and salt to the liquid. Put the garlic through a press and add to the liquid.

2. Arrange layers in a buttered casserole, starting with the beans. Add a layer of chicken, sprinkle with some of the chocolate, and pour some of the liquid over all. Repeat until all the ingredients are used. Top with buttered crumbs.

Bake in a 350° F. oven for about 25 minutes, or until hot and bubbly.

Makes 6 to 8 servings.

CHICKEN BREASTS WITH ALMONDS

4 chicken breasts
Seasoned flour
4 tablespoons chicken fat
or butter
1 onion, sliced
1 can tomatoes
½ cup blanched, chopped
almonds
½ teaspoon ground cinna-
mon

1 ounce chocolate, grated
or put through an elec-
tric blender
½ cup seedless raisins
Salt and pepper to taste
4 cups water or chicken
stock
Fried bread triangles

1. Shake the chicken breasts in a bag of seasoned flour.

2. Melt the fat in a large, heavy skillet. Brown the chicken, re-move it and set it aside.

3. Put the onion in the skillet and simmer until transparent but not brown. Add the tomatoes and cook for 5 minutes more. Strain the sauce, then add the almonds, cinnamon, chocolate, raisins, salt and pepper, and the stock.

4. Return the chicken to the skillet. Pour the sauce over, cover, and simmer until the chicken is tender.

To serve, place the chicken on a hot serving platter. Pour the sauce on top. Surround with fried bread triangles.

Extra sauce may be passed in a sauce boat.

This will make 4 servings.

TURKEY WITH MOLE SAUCE

This is a Mexican dish that will intrigue your guests. No one will be able to guess the ingredients, but all will agree that it is marvelous.

1 turkey (6 pounds)
Water
1 teaspoon salt
¼ to ½ cup olive oil
¼ cup fine dry bread crumbs
2 tablespoons sesame seeds
6 small garlic cloves
3 green peppers
8 ripe fresh tomatoes or canned tomatoes

1 tablespoon chili powder
¼ cup almonds
½ teaspoon ground cinnamon
¼ teaspoon pepper
1 teaspoon salt
2 ounces chocolate (squares, melted, or envelopes)
Boiled rice

1. Have the turkey cut up into serving pieces. Cover with water, add the salt, and bring to a boil. Simmer until the turkey is practically done. This will take from 1 to 1½ hours. Remove the turkey to drain and save the stock.

2. Brown the turkey in olive oil. Place the pieces in a casserole.

3. Put a little olive oil in an electric blender, add the rest of the ingredients except rice, and blend briefly. Turn this into the skillet with the remaining oil, and simmer, stirring, for 5 minutes.

4. Pour enough stock over the turkey to cover it about halfway, and pour the chocolate mixture on top. Cover the casserole.

Bake in a 350° F. oven for 1½ hours.

To serve, remove the turkey pieces to a serving platter and spoon the sauce over it. Surround with boiled rice.

Makes 8 to 10 servings.

SPICY STEWED CHICKEN

1 frying chicken (4 pounds)	Freshly ground pepper to taste
½ cup dry white wine	2 cups water
⅛ teaspoon ground cinnamon	2 ounces chocolate, grated or put through an electric blender
⅛ teaspoon ground cloves	½ cup dried bread crumbs
1 teaspoon salt	¼ cup toasted sesame seeds

1. Cut chicken into serving pieces. Place in a bowl.

2. Mix the wine, cinnamon, cloves, salt, and pepper. Pour this over the chicken. Marinate for 2 hours.

3. Transfer the chicken to a large, heavy skillet. Add the water, chocolate, and bread crumbs to the marinade and pour this over the chicken. Cover. Simmer over low heat until the chicken is tender.

To serve, arrange on a hot serving platter. Sprinkle with the toasted sesame seeds.

This will make 4 servings.

CHICKEN WITH FRUIT

1 frying chicken (4 pounds)	2 ounces semisweet chocolate, grated or put through an electric blender
1 tablespoon chicken fat or butter	1 tablespoon sugar
Seasoned flour	1 teaspoon salt
¼ cup blanched almonds	2 cups water
1 tablespoon sesame seeds	4 tablespoons Curaçao
2 cups canned tomatoes, sieved	2 apples
1 tablespoon red chili powder	2 oranges
⅛ teaspoon ground cinnamon	½ cup pineapple chunks

1. Cut chicken into serving pieces. Shake in a bag with the seasoned flour.

2. Melt fat in a large, heavy skillet, and brown the chicken in it. Remove the chicken and put aside.

3. Put the almonds and the sesame seeds in the fat in the skillet and brown them. Add the sieved tomatoes, chili, cinnamon, chocolate, and sugar. Simmer for 5 minutes and add the salt and water, stirring to mix. Put through the electric blender, and add the Curaçao.

4. Return the chicken to the skillet, pour the sauce over it; cover and simmer until the chicken is tender.

5. Peel, core, and slice the apples. Separate the oranges into sections removing the membranes. Place these two fruits and also the pineapple chunks in the skillet. Cover and continue to simmer just long enough to cook the apples.

To serve, arrange the chicken on a hot serving platter and place the fruit around the edge. Pour the sauce over all.

This makes 4 servings.

INDEX